INSCRIBED
Encounters with the
Ten Commandments

INSCRIBED

Encounters with the Ten Commandments

Rabbi Oren J. Hayon, Editor

With a Foreword by
Andrew Rehfeld, PhD

CENTRAL CONFERENCE OF AMERICAN RABBIS
5780 New York 2020

CCAR Press, 355 Lexington Avenue, New York, NY, 10017
(212) 972-3636
ccarpress@ccarnet.org
www.ccarpress.org

LIBRARY OF CONGRESS CATALOGING-IN-PUBLICATION DATA
Names: Central Conference of American Rabbis, publisher. | Hayon, Oren J,
    1972- editor. | Rehfeld, Andrew, 1965- writer of added foreword.
Title: Inscribed : encounters with the Ten Commandments / Rabbi Oren J.
    Hayon, editor ; with a foreword by Andrew Rehfeld, PhD.
Description: New York : Central Conference of American Rabbis, 5780 = 2020.
    | Summary: "This anthology gives a contemporary perspective by rabbis
    and scholars about each of the Ten Commandments. Each of the
    Commandments has two chapters"-- Provided by publisher.
Identifiers: LCCN 2020003053 (print) | LCCN 2020003054 (ebook) | ISBN
    9780881233391 (trade paperback) | ISBN 9780881233407 (ebook)
Subjects: LCSH: Ten commandments--Criticism, interpretation, etc.
Classification: LCC BS1285.52 .I57 2020 (print) | LCC BS1285.52 (ebook) |
    DDC 222/.1606--dc23
LC record available at https://lccn.loc.gov/2020003053
LC ebook record available at https://lccn.loc.gov/2020003054

Text design and composition
by Scott-Martin Kosofsky
at The Philidor Company,
Rhinebeck, NY

Printed in the United States of America
10 9 8 7 6 5 4 3 2 1

To those I have taught,
and those who have taught me;
To those I have loved,
and those who have loved me.

בְּנִי אִם־חָכַם לִבֶּךָ יִשְׂמַח לִבִּי גַם־אָנִי׃
My child, when your heart gains wisdom,
my heart rejoices also.
—Proverbs 23:15

Contents

Foreword

ANDREW REHFELD, PhD

President, Hebrew Union College–Jewish Institute of Religion

A MODERN READER might be surprised that the Central Conference of American Rabbis would publish a volume entitled *Inscribed: Encounters with the Ten Commandments*. The CCAR was founded in 1889 as the professional association of rabbis affiliated with Reform Judaism, a Judaism that prioritizes reason and rationality as the primary way in which humans are to make sense of God's emergence in our world. By contrast, the very story of the Ten Commandments, the centerpiece of what "Sinai" represents, involves a place we cannot find, at a time we cannot pin down, and a protagonist in Moses who we have no historical evidence of having ever existed.

And yet, such a volume is critically necessary for those seeking to confront foundational issues for Jewish belief, practice, and peoplehood. For whether one takes the story of Sinai to be true as a matter of faith or simply a story that has been retold for twenty-five hundred years or more, the understanding of who we are as a people and our distinct approach to the moral and political world depend on it.

Consider the value of this work by simply reflecting on the main components of its subtitle: "Ten," "Commandments," and "Encounters."

Ten

The necessity of this volume comes first as a simple corrective to those who declare themselves to be "Ten Commandment Jews." Such a claim is frequently made by those who wish to distance themselves from the theological demands of our tradition.

As the first three commandments make clear, the Ten Commandments is a statement about Jewish theology that identifies core features of religious Judaism: God is singular, God is revealed in some manner to humans, and the formation of the Jewish people as a distinct people is itself in some way tied to our understanding of the Ineffable. The idea that one could simultaneously declare oneself to be an atheist *and* "a Ten Commandments Jew" is thus misinformed or simply mistaken. Depending on how one characterizes the fourth commandment to "keep" and "remember" the Sabbath, it would be more accurate to say that these individuals are six or seven commandment Jews!

Commandments

The identification of secular Jews as "Ten Commandment Jews" comes of course from recognizing the strong moral substance of most of the commandments, most of which do not explicitly mention God. Yet their force as commandments stems from their purported origins as coming from God to us via the authority of Moses. The second value of this volume is to force us to consider the role that commands, and authority more generally, play in establishing our ethical obligations.

Moral obligations are generally seen as emanating from two possible sources: the authority of the commander and the content of the command. In the first traditional case, we are obligated to do some action because of the authority of the commander, be that a person or God. Within the confines of most Sinaitic and rabbinic Judaism practiced today (ranging from some forms of Conservative Judaism through Modern Orthodoxy and the various sects of stricter or more separatist Orthodoxy), we are obliged to act *because God commanded us to do so as interpreted by religious authorities*. We need not consider the content of the law or command itself: the fact of our being obliged by an external authority is enough to obligate us.

Enlightenment Judaism shifted from an authoritarian basis of moral action to a second, substantive basis of moral obligation. The very revolution that the Reformers brought about in the nineteenth century and now adopted by all forms of Enlightenment Judaism (including Reform, Reconstructing, and some forms of Conservative Judaism, among others) was to accept instead the moral authority of the individual to make religious and moral decisions. And so, rather than treating our moral obligations as emanating from the authority of others or God, we looked to the value or content of the moral claim itself. As Enlightenment Jews, we refrain from murder not because God or a religious authority told us not to. We refrain from murder because murder is morally wrong.

Most contemporary Jews thus accept in practice some form of Kantian universalism as a non-theological basis of promoting duties and obligations. Having set up the universe in such a way to have moral truth, we are thus forced to ask, what, if anything, does the "commanded-ness" of a moral imperative add to our obligation to perform our duties? Similarly, does it force us to ask, as we do every year on Rosh HaShanah, whether God is bound to this moral universe and whether our obligation is to follow the moral duties we have even when God's command violates them (as it does in the story of the *Akeidah* we read on the holiday). Here, one might say with Kant that we are "commanded" by the very substance of the rule itself in the sense of being obliged by duty to act, a duty derived not by the authority of the commander but by the substance of the claim itself.

Where then does that leave Jewish authorities and God in Reform and other forms of Enlightenment Judaism?

The Reform Jew may believe that it was God who established our moral universe from which emerge correct and incorrect answers to questions of ethics and morality. The Reform Jew may also ask whether God is Godself constrained by moral truth, as much as God would seem to be constrained by analytical or mathematical facts. In any case, the Reform Jew as a matter of practice must rely on rabbis to be teachers, resources, and guides of the highest order, demanding respect for their wisdom and commitment, but stopping well short of investing in them the authority to determine right and wrong.

Encounters

Finally, we can reflect on the very idea of what it means to "encounter" the story of the Ten Commandments. For how do we as

Enlightenment Jews encounter this story when we have no good reason to believe that there ever was a moment of revelation at a place called Sinai, at which God gave these commandments to a person named Moses? The question cuts to the core of how each of us as modern, Reform, and Enlightenment Jews comes to understand the particularity of our tradition, and in particular our relationship with the Source of all being.

What connects Sinaitic and Enlightenment Judaism against secular Judaism is faith in the existence of God as the Source of all being, whatever that means. But what distinguishes Enlightenment Judaism from Sinaitic and rabbinic Judaism is that Enlightenment Judaism refuses to use faith as a basis of evidence in cases that reason and science are capable of judging.

The claim that God gave Torah to Moses at Sinai (of which the Ten Commandments stands as the potent symbol) is a material and historical claim well within the realm of science to test. Since there is not sufficient evidence to demonstrate that there was a historical Moses, let alone that the Jews as a people gathered to receive their law at a specific point in the past, we need not even speculate on whether God was the source of the law itself. Instead Enlightenment Judaism must reject the idea of Sinai as anything except a powerful foundational myth that has shaped the development of the Jewish people for over twenty-five hundred years.

And therein lies the singular value of this volume to all people no matter if they are Sinaitic, Enlightenment, or secular Jews. For the story of the Ten Commandments has come to identify core features and themes of the Jewish people that have sustained us for thousands of years.

Encountering the Ten Commandments means confronting questions of theology, morality, and political formation. The essays here serve as a powerful way to encounter these core features of our people. We thus welcome this volume from the Central Conference of American Rabbis as a perfect illustration of the role that rabbis play to help us confront the most important questions we have as Jews.

Introduction

Rabbi Oren J. Hayon

*The tablets were inscribed on both their surfaces: they were
inscribed on the one side and on the other.*
—Exodus 32:15

*How were the Ten Commandments given? Five were inscribed
on one tablet and stood opposite the five inscribed on the other
tablet, so that each of the commandments faced another.*
—M'chilta D'Rabbi Yishmael 20:14

Students of classical Rabbinic text will be familiar with
the Sages' well-known assertion that Torah existed even before God
had begun to create the universe. It is a patently outrageous claim,
of course, to suggest that Torah literally transcends time and space
and that a *book*, of all things, predated the existence of the entire
cosmos. Unconstrained by reason, however, the Rabbis posit that
not only did Torah exist before Creation, but God could not have
accomplished the work of Creation without Torah, consulting it
for guidance as a construction worker relies upon an architectur-
al blueprint. It is an extravagant spiritual claim to suggest that the
Torah's words—whether spoken or heard, revealed or discovered—
are the scaffolding on which everything we know is built. But one of
the benefits of living in relationship with Torah is the peculiar way in
which it helps one feel comfortable with spiritual extravagance.

Torah (by which I mean not merely a parchment scroll, nor the
Five Books of Moses calligraphed on it, but the way in which it
stands synecdochically for Jewish learning in every form) is the

foundational phenomenon of Jewish existence. For Jews, the study of Torah is unlike any other sort of study; we undertake it not to absorb new facts or acquire new skills. Instead, learning is *itself* an act of devotion. The purpose of Jewish study is not to memorize holy text, but to continually explore it more deeply, to discover new angles from which one can approach it, to collect it like a rare and precious element, to carry it into the rooms where one lives and hold it up to the light.

Every engaged Jewish life is undergirded by Torah. Irrespective of one's ritual observance, customs, or beliefs, the Jew is never isolated from Torah. In Judaism, the cycle of learning and teaching never ceases to churn, neither on earth nor in the infinite noumenal realms beyond us. But is there a single point at which its headwaters flow into human experience? And if so, what is the first primal encounter of Torah where human learners meet their transcendent Teacher?

If we want to identify a specific biblical moment when the universe first encounters the Holy One as *notein hatorah*, the "Giver of Torah," we might identify Genesis 1:3. There, God speaks for the first time in the Bible, declaring, *y'hi or!*—"Let there be light!" Or perhaps we might point to a moment that comes soon afterward, in verse 28, when God first speaks to human beings, commanding them, *p'ru ur'vu*—"Be fruitful and multiply." But it is not until later in the biblical epic when God first begins participating personally in the endeavor of Torah, when God's commanding presence generates and disseminates law to an audience of eager learners: the theophany at Sinai. There, for the first time, Israel is gathered as a people and a nation to receive Torah, and for the first time God's people agrees to a set of laws and instructions by which they will live.

The revelation of the Ten Commandments is the formative moment in the life of the Jewish people, when law, peoplehood, theology, and morality are conceived simultaneously amid thunder, smoke, and the seismic blast of *shofarot*. The Ten Commandments (which, since not all of them are strictly "commandments," may be better described by the Hebrew phrase *Aseret Hadibrot*, the "Ten

Utterances") have not only attained prominence as practical guides for spiritual living; they have acquired a unique veneration in American society and occupy an enormous parcel of cultural and academic real estate in our modern lives.

Rabbi Abraham Joshua Heschel famously suggested that the entire Hebrew Bible is essentially a midrash about God's revelation of commandments at Sinai.[1] It may logically follow from this assertion that all of Jewish existence is a commentary on the identity of a God, whose speech knits divinity into human life. Each Jewish decision we make in everyday life—about how to raise our children, how to conduct ourselves at work, how to participate in the lives of our communities—represents a choice about how we interpret Torah's meaning and relevance in our lives; our daily existence becomes a midrashic response to the commanding voice that originated at Sinai. And so, when in synagogues today communities of worshipers rise to their feet to hear the ritual recitation of the Ten Commandments on *Shabbat Yitro*, they personally embody an unbroken, timeless circle that contains study, worship, and peoplehood.

The Torah's narratives of Creation and the redemption from slavery comprise pivotal gestures of covenant that enact God's authority over and concern for Israel. The giving of the Ten Commandments fulfills a theological purpose that is similar to the ones achieved by those other two decisive moments in Israel's history, but Sinai adds an additional component not present either in Eden or on the shores of the Reed Sea: only there does the connection between heaven and earth require the people's response and assent. The Ten Commandments were given directly to the people; if they are to endure, the people must accept their role as the caretakers of God's sacred utterances. In this sense, *all* of Jewish learning and insight is *torah sheb'al peh*, "Oral Torah." Every one of the world's teachers and learners are simultaneously Torah's consumers and its creators. Torah was not simply received from on high in a single dramatic moment; the conversation between the Torah and its teachers unfolds in an ongoing cycle I call "collaborative revelation." God's self unfurls through the countless ways in which Torah is studied and interpreted over the

years and across the globe. Our engagement with Torah produces yet
more Torah, which in turn offers itself up for new study and examination: an ever-new Torah unspooling in endless fractal coils.

This book reflects one of Judaism's long-standing affirmations:
shiv'im panim latorah—the Torah may be compared to a priceless,
seventy-faceted jewel. Embedded in this charming metaphor is an
unmistakable acknowledgment that Jewish learning encodes within
itself a commitment to plurality of thought and belief. The enterprise of Jewish study cannot begin before a student learns to revere
intellectual diversity and the precious truth that every learner
approaches the text from one's own unique interpretive angle.

In this collection, each of the Ten Commandments is presented in
a pair of essays by contributors representing a wide variety of back-
grounds. These authors reflect a broad range of religious beliefs and
professional specialization: in chaplaincy, law, technology, journal-
ism, social activism, and the armed services. They live all across the
United States and serve many different sorts of communities and
constituents. I am proud that their contributions to this volume help
showcase the diversity of thought, the rigor of scholarship, and the
spirit of entrepreneurial learning that flourishes in today's Jewish
world.

What I find most delightful about the volume we have produced
together is its multivocality. Though all of the essays were written
individually, with no coordination between their authors, their jux-
taposition places them into a new conversation with each other. This
is, of course, also true of Jewish commentary in its most classic form,
where each interpretive voice is drawn into dialogue with all others.
Our Sages taught that "Torah is only acquired in fellowship," and
I am deeply grateful to the friends, colleagues, and teachers whose
work fills these pages and who have been a constant source of inspiration. Exploring our contributors' words and their expertise through
countless back-and-forth exchanges has been an unexpectedly precious and holy *shakla v'tarya*, "give and take," during the process of
assembling this book. My discussions with them have revealed new

strata of religious discovery and enlightenment that I would never have encountered had they not participated in this project.

The epigraph from the Rabbinic midrashic collection *M'chilta D'Rabbi Yishmael* with which our book opens suggests that in addition to the intersecting and overlapping layers of textual commentary from across thousands of miles and dozens of centuries, the Torah engages in a perpetual dialogue *with itself*. As a Reform rabbi, I am delighted that this collection of essays will amplify, ever so slightly, the Torah's ongoing internal monologue. I take a special measure of pride in the way this book exemplifies our movement's eager participation in collaborative revelation, as an expression of its conviction that Torah must always remain relevant to human life. It is deeply fulfilling to know that its publication will refract some of the light from the Torah's seventy facets onto the pages studied by progressive Jewish learners, whose numbers—thank God—are growing each day, in ways that our teachers and ancestors could never have imagined.

This book enters the world at an exhilarating time for Jewish study. In synagogues across the denominational spectrum, the spirituality of learning is reaffirmed when *b'nei mitzvah* come of age, at confirmation rituals where teen learners' maturation is bound together with their community's observance of *chag matan torateinu*, Shavu'ot, and at weekly *parashat hashavua* classes experiences where each year brings a new opportunity to experience the phenomenon of Sinai anew. And increasing numbers of progressive Jews are embracing Jewish text in exciting, accessible new ways beyond synagogues' walls as well: at educational conferences, liberal *yeshivot*, and *batei midrash*; at study groups and book clubs; and in robust online communities that utilize groundbreaking new digital tools. It is my hope that this volume will be a helpful resource for those who have come to cherish, as I do, the affirming embrace of scholarship, fellowship, and the dazzling shimmer of Torah's perennial bloom.

NOTES

1 Abraham Joshua Heschel, *God in Search of Man: A Philosophy of Judaism* (Philadelphia: Jewish Publication Society, 1955), 185.

Acknowledgments

As with every publication, this book could not have come into being without the dedicated labor of many devoted and hardworking professionals. First and foremost, I want to acknowledge, with deepest gratitude and admiration, the support and stewardship of my friend and teacher Rabbi Hara Person. Through no merit of my own, I have received a double portion of blessing by getting the opportunity to work with Hara as she held two vital positions: first, as the CCAR Press's lead publisher; and now, as she exercises brave, capable, and visionary leadership as the chief executive of the CCAR. Hara exemplifies the noblest and most vital priorities of our movement: erudition and scholarship, principled ethics and virtue, and an unwavering commitment to improving and deepening Reform Jewish life in America and around the world. It has been an honor to work with her on this project. The publication of *Inscribed* also introduced me to my editor Rabbi Sonja K. Pilz, PhD, with whom I built a wonderful relationship during the course of our work together. The book's strongest asset was Sonja's faith in it, and she lovingly shepherded our manuscript from beginning to end in a uniquely gentle, supportive, and encouraging manner. I owe her a great debt of gratitude—and a measure of apology, as well: for my unceasingly busy schedule that kept her waiting far too frequently. Sonja's sensitivity to language and her facility with the complex choreography of editing and publishing are inspiring and delightful, and I have loved sharing this work with her.

There are a number of other dedicated members of the CCAR Press staff whose behind-the-scenes work were vital as well: Deborah Smilow, Sasha Smith, Leta Cunningham, and Raquel Fairweather; CCAR interns Vanessa Harper and Gabriel Snyder; and copy editor Debra Corman, designer Scott-Martin Kosofsky, proofreader

Michelle Kwitkin, and cover designer Barbara Leff. All of them contributed in large and small ways to help breathe life into this book, and they have my thanks.

Additionally, I want to acknowledge the members of the *Inscribed* advisory committee and their helpful support along the way: Rabbi Joshua L. Caruso, Rabbi Micah Citrin, Rabbi Wendi Geffen, Rabbi Shana R. Goldstein, Rabbi Debra L. Kassof, Rabbi Peter S. Knobel, PhD, *z"l*, Rabbi Joel M. Mosbacher, Rabbi Brigitte S. Rosenberg, and Rabbi David B. Thomas. This group was convened to assist in helping to shape the large contours of the book. They were a great asset in the work of identifying authors to contribute material, and their wise counsel was an invaluable aid as the book's final form took shape.

The process of assembling this book made many demands on my schedule and my mental energy, and it would never have been possible without the loving and encouraging support of my wonderful home community at Congregation Emanu El in Houston. Our congregation has a long and distinguished legacy of Jewish learning and a strong dedication to supporting the work of scholarship within the Reform Movement, and so I am hopeful that this book will bring a special measure of pride and fulfillment to our community. I am thankful to Emanu El's many members, who have been encouraging during this book's production and understanding about its demands on my schedule, and I am particularly indebted to our unparalleled staff team, whose daily work makes Emanu El an enriching and supportive Jewish home for so many. I must make special mention of the dear clergy colleagues with whom I work most closely: Rabbi Pamela B. Silk, Rabbi Joshua Fixler, Rabbi Roy A. Walter, and Cantor Rollin Simmons, all of whom bring soulful compassion and care to the holy work they do each day with our congregation. My partnership with them is truly joyful and represents a primary source of ongoing revelation and inspiration in my life.

Finally, I must express my love and gratitude to my family. Their nearness blesses me at all times with grace and goodness—assuredly more than I deserve. I am deeply grateful that my mother is a daily presence in our family's life and in our home; her closeness brings strength and delight to us all. No less influential is the precious memory of my beloved father Yehiel, *alav hashalom*, which even in his absence provides tender comfort and valuable inspiration. I am inexpressibly thankful to my wife, Julie, for her steadfast love and support and for her willingness to have shared a rewarding but unpredictable journey with me for more than twenty years. Our partnership has been a great gift to me, and its value is far greater than I can describe in these few lines.

But my most joyful blessing comes from my children. A well-known midrash (*Shir Hashirim Rabbah* 1:3) recounts a dialogue between the Israelites and God, during which the two parties negotiate the terms under which the Torah will be given to humanity. God rejects one proposal after another, arguing that Israel has failed to provide a reliable guarantor for the Torah's safekeeping. God remains unwilling to finalize the agreement until the Israelites present a final offer: their children will be the Torah's guarantors. At last, God is convinced and agrees to grant the Torah to Israel as its eternal possession.

The midrash affirms a truth that I have come to know firsthand: both through parenthood and through Torah can we come to know God's immanence and merit a taste of eternality. When we commit ourselves simultaneously to spiritual learning and to the well-being of the generation that will follow us, we arrive at a reassuring confidence about the world's future. This is, I think, why the blessing following a congregational reading of Torah reminds us that a primary dividend of Jewish learning is חַיֵּי עוֹלָם נָטַע בְּתוֹכֵנוּ—eternal life implanted within. As a teacher of Torah, and as a parent of children who fill me with hope, I feel breathlessly grateful for the promises they offer: promises of goodness and mercy, of justice and forgiveness, of righteousness and truth everlasting.

FIRST COMMANDMENT

אָנֹכִי יהוה אֱלֹהֶיךָ אֲשֶׁר הוֹצֵאתִיךָ
מֵאֶרֶץ מִצְרַיִם מִבֵּית עֲבָדִים:

*I the Eternal am your God who brought you out
of the land of Egypt, the house of bondage.*
—Exodus 20:2

God's Identity

Perspectives from Jewish Philosophy

RABBI KARI HOFMAISTER TULING, PhD

THE TEN COMMANDMENTS open with a statement: "I am the Eternal your God." What does that mean?

According to the great medieval legal giant Moses Maimonides, this statement is actually a commandment, and it commands us to feel a sense of awe toward God. As he writes in the *Mishneh Torah*, "It is a precept to love and fear this revered and awe-inspiring God."[1] This idea has certain implications for us. "What is the way of acquiring love and fear of God?" Maimonides asks. In his view, it is an intellectual act: we should engage in contemplation of God. In Maimonides's view, God is completely transcendent, approachable through the intellect, especially through scientific inquiry.

Let us think about this idea in modern/postmodern philosophical terms, using the theological works of Abraham Joshua Heschel as our example.

Heschel suggests that we encounter God in the realm of the ineffable, a realm that surpasses our ability to categorize and name, a realm that is separate from our everyday world.[2] In fact, Heschel argues that in the realm of the ineffable, we completely lose our sense of self. That is to say, when we encounter the Divine, we do not meet God in an "I-Thou" relationship—or even an "I-It" relationship—because in the midst of this encounter we no longer possess a separate and independent "I."

In this context, we can no longer differentiate ourselves from the rest of Creation—nor can we differentiate moments in time. In some sense, the categories of space and time collapse and lose their significance. As a result of this shift in awareness, "things surrounding us emerge from the triteness with which we have endowed them, and their strangeness opens like a void between them and our mind, a void that no words can fill."[3]

What does that mean, in the context of the philosophical conversations of its time? What is at issue here is a concept the phenomenologists call "categorial intuition"—or, more precisely, the issue is what kind of truth emerges from categorial intuition. The founder of phenomenology, Edmund Husserl, coined this term to identify the specific kind of awareness articulated when one makes a declarative statement such as "this paper is white." What might seem to be a rather straightforward assertion is in fact a specific kind of insight into a given state of affairs.

In his *Logical Investigations,*[4] Husserl provides a nuanced explanation of what is meant by this phrase. We see the "paper" and its "whiteness," but we do not see it "being"—for this predicative form capturing the state of affairs is a categorial intuition. In the case of the white paper, the object and its attribute are both visible, but the state of affairs itself, the "paper-being-white," is not. We do not perceive this categorial intuition through our senses. It is an intuitive insight into a given state of affairs.

In Martin Heidegger's view, on the other hand, phrases such as "this paper is white" or "the chair is yellow" imply both *being as relational factor of the state of affairs as such and being as truth-relation.*"[5] When we encounter an object in its givenness, we name and categorize it. We are taking in the given state of affairs (such as the chair-being-yellow) and making a truth-assertion on that basis ("this chair is yellow").

In suggesting the realm of the ineffable, therefore, Heschel is arguing against Heidegger's confidence in our ability to categorize and make truth-judgments regarding a given state of affairs. As Heschel writes, "Analyze, weigh and measure a tree as you please, observe and describe its form and functions, its genesis and the laws to which it is subject; still an *acquaintance* with its *essence* never comes about."[6] In other words, the judgment that "this object is a tree" does not get us any closer to its true meaning, because naming is not the same thing as understanding.

We make do with the fact that these names might not capture the fullness of the experience. This inability to articulate is particularly pronounced in the realm of the ineffable: it is a radiance that cannot be adequately subsumed under our existing names.

But to take the counterview, how is it that our weighing and measuring of an object does not bring us closer to acquaintance with its essence? Are we not able to recognize that each of these new viewpoints relates back to this same object, and in so doing, are we not enlarging our understanding of it? And how can we be certain that this object has any kind of transcendent meaning, alluding to the realm of the ineffable, which lies beyond the reach of our descriptions?

According to Heidegger, in the act of simple perception, we have an awareness that it is the same object even if we were to view it from another angle. When I look at a table from the top and then from the bottom, I know that it is the same table, despite the very different appearance that the two viewpoints offer.

Heidegger argues that we do not first perceive the table from above and below and then afterward create a synthesis of these two views to establish that the table is one and the same. Rather, it is given to us continuously in our perception.

But Heidegger's approach is not shared by all phenomenologists. Husserl makes a fine distinction in his *Sixth Investigation*, in that he resists collapsing the object and its perception together as a "full perception of the thing." As he writes:

> I see a thing, e.g. this box, but I do not see my sensations. I always see *one and the same box*, however *it* may be turned and tilted. I have always the *same* "content of consciousness." . . . Very different contents are therefore experienced, though the same object is perceived. The experienced content, generally speaking, is not the perceived object.[7]

Each view is not a full perception of the thing itself, but rather it is a full perception of the *experienced content*. Each view is a full perception of *our experience of the box* as it appears to us in that moment—but it is not a full perception of the box itself. The thing itself does not fully reveal itself in each glance; it is only partially disclosed.

When we see the object in a series of disclosures—such as turning a small box over in our hand—we will synthesize these views into a whole, so that we can imagine the other side of the box despite its hiddenness.

But, as Husserl argues, our naming it as a box might in fact cause us to gloss over some aspect of its particularity. We might assume, for example, that because it is red on this side it must be red all around—even though that assumption might not be true—and even if we were never to turn it over, we would always think of it as "the red box."

Unlike Heidegger, who asserts that a single view is in itself a full perception of the thing, Husserl argues that our view of the object—whether we view it just once or we view it an infinite number of times—is never a full perception of the thing and never fully yields the object's essence. We only have access to our experience of the object as it gives itself to us in that moment.

To return to our example of a box-being-red: Heidegger would argue that having encountered an object that conforms to our category of "box" and that is the color we have named as "red," we may make the true judgment that "this box is red," a statement that is true in the context of that particular moment in time. Even if the box was later proved to be a different color (perhaps we made a mistake due to poor lighting, or perhaps we were not aware that the other side was white), the assertion "this box is red" was true then, at the time when we made it.

Husserl, on the other hand, would argue that the judgment "this box is red" is not true; rather, if we are approaching the event with phenomenological rigor, then we may only assert that "the content of my experience is that this box is red." If it were possible to assemble an infinite number of sightings of this box and all the various appearances of its possible redness, then we could establish the truth of its color. In that sense, the judgment "this box is red" is an approximation of the truth.

In this context, it is not difficult to see how Heschel can assert the possibility of the realm of the ineffable: Heschel follows Husserl. Our perception of the world involves the interplay of presence and absence, of articulate speech and silent wonder. We do not ever capture its fullness.

According to Heschel, when we let go of our categories, that is when we are able to encounter transcendent meaning. As Heschel writes:

> We are able to exploit, to label things with well-trimmed words; but when ceasing to subject them to our purposes and to impose on them the forms of our intellect, we are stunned and incapable of saying what things are in themselves; it is an experience of being unable to experience something we face: too great to be perceived. Music, poetry, religion—they all initiate in the soul's encounter with an aspect of reality for which reason has no concepts and language has no names.[8]

To understand the full weight of this statement, compare it against Heidegger's assertion: "It is not so much that we see the objects and things but rather that we first talk about them. To put it more precisely: we do not say what we see, but rather the reverse, we see what *one says* about the matter."[9] For Heidegger, humanity is the source of all meaning in the world. Heschel would retort, "Meaning is not man's gift to reality."[10]

We are not the full measure of all things, according to Heschel, nor are we the origin of their significance. In fact, this emphasis on our capacity to name and categorize might push us away from apprehending the truth, in Heschel's estimation. We encounter meaning when we drop our categories and our names and simply abandon ourselves to wonder.

According to Heschel, God enters the world through our deeds—but not directly; rather, it is through an effulgence of God's glory that overfills us and transports us beyond the narrow confines of exclusive self-concern. In encountering it, we lose our sense of self and transcend our experience of being-in-the-world—which is why we cannot speak from the perspective of the "I" when we are caught up in it.

In this context, we are no longer beings who use tools and create our own meanings for the objects in the world; rather, we become the objects in God's world, or rather, objects of God's thought. In that sense, we step outside of time and come into contact with that which is eternal. In other words, we do not create this meaning in our lives; rather, the meaning of the world predates us.

According to Maimonides, the first commandment is the demand that we love and fear God. That experience of love and fear is rooted in our intellectual apprehension of God's effect upon the world. For Maimonides, however, we do not ever fully understand God or know God's essence. There is an aspect that always eludes our grasp.

We learned that for Heschel, too, this elusiveness means that we must acknowledge that there is a transcendent meaning to the world, a meaning that we did not create ourselves. In line with Husserl, Heschel argued against the idea that we can name reality and bestow meaning upon it. Rather, he suggested, we encounter God in a nameless place, in a realm beyond our categories. Therefore, when we read "I am the Eternal your God" as the first of the commandments, we must approach this expression with humility: the idea that God exists is indeed a revelation.

NOTES

1   Maimonides, *Mishneh Torah, Yesodei HaTorah* (literally "The Foundations of Torah") 2:1, quoted in Nehama Leibowitz, *Studies in Devarim/Deuteronomy* (Jerusalem: Haomanim Press, n.d.), 66.

2   Abraham Joshua Heschel, *Man Is Not Alone: A Philosophy of Religion* (New York: Noonday Press, 1994).

3   Heschel, *Man Is Not Alone*, 39.

4   Edmund Husserl, *Logical Investigations* (Abington-on-Thames: Routledge, 2001).

5   Martin Heidegger, *History of the Concept of Time*, trans. Theodore Kisiel (Bloomington: Indiana University Press, 1985), 54.

6   Heschel, *Man Is Not Alone*, 6.

7   Edmund Husserl, *Logical Investigations*, vol. 2, trans. J. N. Findlay (New York: Humanities Press, 1970), 565.

8   Heschel, *Man Is Not Alone*, 36.

9   Heidegger, *History of the Concept of Time*, 56.

10 Heschel, *Man Is Not Alone*, 28.

Revelation as Conversation

RABBI JOSHUA FEIGELSON, PhD

WHAT HAPPENS WHEN two or more people have a conversation? Many things *can* happen, of course. But when things are going well, we might agree with the twentieth-century German philosopher Hans-Georg Gadamer: "In a successful conversation [both parties . . .] are bound to one another in a new community. . . . [We are] transformed into a communion in which we do not remain what we were."[1] In a true conversation, the encounter isn't merely an exchange of information, but something more than that. All of the parties involved feel a sense of agency and responsibility for the conversation itself. They are able to make space for each other, challenge one another with respect and sensitivity, and ultimately sustain the conversation. In the process, they become connected and part of something larger than the sum of its previous parts.

That conversation, held and nurtured by the conversation partners, reflects three dimensions: first, each of the parties in the conversation acknowledges the agency and legitimacy of the other partners, as well as their own; second, that acknowledgment builds trust between the conversation partners; third, the feeling of trust and understanding leads the participants in the conversation to a changed sense of who they are, individually and collectively.

In this essay I will argue that the first of the Ten Commandments grounds revelation in a fundamental paradigm of conversation and that by understanding revelation this way, we can understand the relationship between God and the Jewish people within each of these three dimensions: agency, trust, and communion.

Anochi Adonai Elohecha: "I the Eternal am your God who brought you out of the land of Egypt, the house of bondage." Traditional commentators have tended to focus on two aspects of this verse: First, there is the question, "In what sense can it be considered a commandment along the lines of the other nine?" Second, "What is the nature of the very first word, *Anochi*, 'I'?" However, equally noteworthy is the third word, *Elohecha*. Unlike in many other passages in the Torah, God here does not only say "I am the Eternal," but rather speaks to the Israelites in the second person: "I the Eternal am *your* God who brought *you* out of Egypt." In fact, throughout the Ten Commandments, God addresses the Israelites directly in the second person: "*You* shall have no other gods besides Me; *you* shall remember the Sabbath day; *you* shall not murder," etc. From the outset, God is talking to the Israelites and, by extension, to us—their descendants—hearing and reading the text. God is speaking to us, and that, of course, is the first precondition for a conversation: one of the parties needs to speak.

Is it really a conversation at this point? On one level, it is: the people verbally respond to God's words with *naaseh v'nishma*, "We will do and we will hear" (Exodus 24:7). On another level, however, we are inclined to doubt how much of a true conversation this really is. As the Babylonian Talmudic sage Rav Acha bar Yaakov observed, the Torah would seem to have been accepted under duress: if the Almighty is the one making the offer of a relationship, how could the people realistically say no, particularly after all that God had done for them?[2] If this was a conversation, it was not one between two equal parties.

Rava famously answers Rav Acha by pointing to the Jewish people's reacceptance of the Torah in the time of Esther—a period when God was less visible (remember that Esther is the only book of the Bible that does not mention God). As Rabbi Yitz Greenberg observed in his 1982 essay "The Third Great Cycle of Jewish History," the people's recommitment at this time reflected the relationship of two mature parties.[3] The conversational relationship gained legitimacy as God made space for the people; and consequently, the people took greater responsibility and asserted greater voice. This dynamic only gained force as God became increasingly removed from Jewish history after the destruction of the Second Temple in Jerusalem, the end of sacrifices and prophecy, and the rise of Rabbinic Judaism. All of these dynamics made greater room for humans, put them on a more equal footing with God, and made them fuller members of the eternal conversation.

That conversation continues throughout Jewish history until today, as Jews pray, perform mitzvot, study Torah, meditate, and in countless other ways seek to hear and respond to God's voice. Each of us—including me as I write this and you as you read it—is a participant in what contemporary writer Parker Palmer defines as truth: "An eternal conversation about things that matter, conducted with passion and discipline."[4] We are custodians of that eternal conversation, kindling a flame that was originally lit in the fiery cloud surrounding Mount Sinai at the moment of revelation.

Agency

A genuine conversation requires that all parties be able to freely enter and exit. As we have already observed, while the original conversation at Sinai may not have satisfied this criterion, over time greater parity emerged. The Shoah, however, posed a new challenge to the conversation: if God was not only withdrawn from Jewish history, but seemingly utterly absent, was (is) it possible to say that a conversation was (is) still taking place? This was the central challenge to post-Shoah Jewish thought. Greenberg, whom we have already mentioned, provided one of the more provocative responses: After the Shoah, the conversation between the Jewish people and God is in fact at its most mature stage, as the Jewish people reaffirm the covenant out of their own free will. Though the authority of the covenant was broken, "the Jewish people, released from its obligations, chose voluntarily to take it on again. . . . God was no longer in a position to command, but the Jewish people was so in love with the dream of redemption that it volunteered to carry on its mission."[5] Or, as Greenberg puts it later in his essay, "In every covenantal

relationship"—which, for our purposes, I would assert is synony-
mous with a genuine conversation—"the partners must ultimately
choose between quality and force. True love can only exist when the
imbalance of power has been overcome by redistribution of power
or, in God's case, by a binding renunciation of using the imbalance."[6]

We are therefore living in an age when the conversation, though
being much more difficult because of God's seeming hiddenness,
is potentially much more mature for the same reason. It is a more
nuanced conversation, one in which we have to look and listen in
unobvious places to find our conversation partner. But this is simultaneously an age when God invites us to exercise our own voice;
when, perhaps, God is listening more closely, even if God is seemingly unwilling to intervene in history.

Trust

If agency of all parties is the precondition for genuine conversation,
trust is both its by-product and the condition for the conversation's
continuation. Likewise, Jewish thought has long recognized the
trusting leap of faith that God takes not only at the moment of revelation, but even in the very act of creating humans and the world:
"Rabbi Shimon said, 'When the Holy One was about to create the first
human, the ministering angels formed themselves into factions and
groups. Some of them said, 'Let him be created.' Some of them said,
'Let him not be created.'"[7] The risk of creating humans, of course, is
our propensity for evil. But God seemingly sees that risk outweighed
by our possibility for good: our capacity for lying is outweighed by
our capacity for loving-kindness; our capacity for conflict is counter-
vailed by our capacity for justice. Fundamentally, God trusts us to do
more good than evil.

That trust grows as the conversation continues. In one of the Talmud's most famous stories, the Rabbis tell the Divine Voice that it
may not interfere in their debate: "Rabbi Natan encountered Elijah
the prophet and said to him, 'What did the Holy Blessed One do at
that time?' Elijah said, 'The Holy Blessed One smiled and said: My
children have triumphed over Me; My children have triumphed over

Me.'"[8] This does not mean that God does not have a place in the eternal conversation—after all, God's word, the Torah, is the touchstone for a conversation spanning millennia. However, in order to make room for a maturing human voice, God is getting out of the way. In a post-Shoah world, God remains a part of the conversation in more subtle ways; the nature of the trust between God and the Jewish people has changed. Just as children and parents have one kind of conversation based on a particular kind of trust, and adult parents and children have a different kind of conversation based on a different kind of trust, the nature of the trust at the heart of the covenantal conversation between God and the Jewish people evolves over time.

The violation of trust shatters the conversational dynamic and requires repair if the conversation is to continue. When the Israelites violate the covenant by worshiping the Golden Calf, Moses engages God in conversation to ask for forgiveness and a re-establishment of trust. This episode becomes the paradigm for our annual ritual of forgiveness, Yom Kippur, when the violations of trust that erode our capacity to sustain the eternal conversation are addressed and remedied. As the Mishnah notes, "For transgressions between a person and their fellow, Yom Kippur does not affect atonement until they has pacified their fellow"[9]—that is, had a conversation and asked for forgiveness. The same conversation that we have with our "fellows" we have, individually and collectively, with God. It is through conversation that trust is restored and maintained.

"A Communion in Which We Do Not Remain What We Were"
In Gadamer's paradigm for conversation with which I opened this essay, he posits that "in a successful conversation [both parties . . .] are bound to one another in a new community. . . . [We are] transformed into a communion in which we do not remain what we were."[10] Unquestionably, the Israelites, and we as their descendants, were transformed through the encounter at Sinai. We became "a kingdom of priests and a holy nation" (Exodus 19:6) and "a people consecrated to the Eternal" (Deuteronomy 14:2). Through the acceptance of Torah by our forefathers and foremothers and its

continual reacceptance generation after generation, indeed day after day, we are made new and renewed. Every encounter we have with Torah, with the mitzvot of our rituals, traditions, and laws—at each and every moment we re-engage the covenant and add a new element to the *ner tamid*, the "eternal flame" of conversation.

But it is not only we who are transformed. "If you follow My laws and faithfully observe My commandments . . . I will establish My abode in your midst, and I will not spurn you. I will be ever present in your midst: I will be your God, and you shall be My people" (Leviticus 26:3, 11–12). With every act we take to stay in the eternal conversation, with every mitzvah we perform, God is renewed alongside us, and the conversation is sustained. God, too, becomes something new with every interaction. Contra the medieval philosophers who insisted on God's unchanging nature, the Torah is full of sources that suggest that God, in God's relationship with human beings in general and the Jewish people in particular, is a learning and growing being, just as we are. God learns about human limitations and foibles, as well as the human capacities for love, justice, and mercy. God learns to self-limit, to ask questions, to listen. In short, God learns to be a partner in conversation with us.

Conclusion

How might our lives change if we view our relationship with God not as that of commander and soldiers, but of a conversation partner in an eternal conversation with us? I will end by offering three potential implications. First, I think it is easier to live with the idea of God as a listener. In a post-Shoah, climate-changing world, when God's presence seems more hidden than ever, the notion of God as our conversation partner enables me to conceive of God as listening to me individually and to us collectively. Second, it invites us to listen even more closely for God. Especially in a world in which nationalism, including Jewish religious nationalism, can generate a dangerously illusory sense of God's presence, imagining God as a conversation partner demands that we listen attentively for what is really being said and that we remain humble enough not to claim that we have grasped the fullness of what our interlocutor is trying to say.

Finally, remembering that we are all created in God's image, I think the notion of God as conversation partner suggests how we should treat our fellow Jews and fellow human beings. To paraphrase the Talmudic sage Abba Shaul:[11] Just as God lives in an eternal conversation with us, so, too, are we in eternal conversation with the images of God. The virtues of recognizing one another's agency, of engendering trust and repairing it when it is violated, and of opening ourselves to be transformed through our encounters—these are of course paradigms not only for our relationship with the Divine, but for our relationship with our fellow humans as well.

NOTES

1 H. G. Gadamer, *Truth and Method* (New York: Seabury Press, 1975), 371.
2 Babylonian Talmud, *Shabbat* 88a.
3 Irving Greenberg, *The Third Great Cycle of Jewish History* (New York: CLAL, 1982).
4 Parker J. Palmer, *The Courage to Teach: Exploring the Inner Landscape of a Teacher's Life* (San Francisco: Jossey-Bass, 1998), 130.
5 Irving Greenberg, *Voluntary Covenant* (New York: CLAL, 1982).
6 Greenberg, *Voluntary Covenant*
7 *B'reishit Rabbah* 8:5.
8 *Babylonian Talmud, Bava M'tzia* 59b.
9 *Mishnah Yoma* 8:9.
10 Gadamer, *Truth and Method*
11 *Babylonian Talmud, Shabbat* 133b.

Israel's History of Enslavement as a Prerequisite for Revelation

Elsie R. Stern, PhD

THE IDEA that the Israelites were slaves in the land of Egypt has been central to Jewish identity since the early beginnings of a Jewish narrative. The texts of our biblical canon repeatedly assert that we were slaves in the land of Egypt and that God redeemed us from there. Our Rabbinic Sages made this narrative central to our prayers, and the theme has remained crucial to the self-understanding of many Jews—even those Jews who do not espouse many other aspects of traditional Jewish identity and belief.

In the past several decades, though, scholars of ancient Israelite history have largely overturned the assumption that this story reflects a historical reality. In all probability, our ancestors did not leave Egypt; instead, ancient Israel emerged from people living in the land of Canaan, which was under Egyptian control for much of the second millennium BCE. In other words, our ancestors were subject to Egypt's regional power, but were not, as individuals, slaves in Egypt. The story of slavery and the Exodus is more myth than history.

While the assertion that "the Exodus didn't happen" can be disconcerting, the change in status from history to myth has had little impact on the centrality of the story for Jewish identity. For millennia, we have consciously taken on the identity of former slaves, even as we acknowledge that this identity does not reflect our personal, historical experience. In the words of the Haggadah, we commit to regarding ourselves *k'ilu* ("as though") we ourselves had been redeemed from Egypt and to living our lives grounded in that self-perception. As Rabbi Kelilah Miller said when she was a student at the Reconstructionist Rabbinical College, "[Before learning that the Exodus wasn't historical] I had thought that one generation *were* slaves that had been redeemed from Egypt and that for all subsequent generations it was a '*k'ilu*' experience. Now I know that it has been a '*k'ilu*' experience from the start." Our personal assumption of the identity of redeemed slaves has always been an act of imagination and will.

But why do we continue to take on this identity, generation after generation? The tenacity of the Exodus story attests to its status as myth, rather than misunderstanding of history or "fake news." A myth is a story that articulates truths that may or may not be demonstrated by historical experience. The Exodus story sticks because many of us feel that the story of enslavement and freedom is true to our experience in an essential way, even if the events of the Exodus plot are not part of our lived experience, or even that of our ancestors.

For millennia, the Exodus story has resonated both with Jewish collective historical and political experiences and with individual existential and spiritual experiences. In addressing the question "Why did the Exodus story become so central to biblical literature?" biblical scholar Peter Machinist has pointed out that the redactors of the biblical collection were ethnic Judeans who had emigrated to Judea from where their ancestors had been exiled in the early sixth century BCE. For these people, whose ancestors had been exiled and who were returning to Judea to build a society centered around the worship of the Eternal, the Exodus story resonated strongly. While they had not been slaves in Egypt, they *had* been part of the exiled community in Babylonia. They understood their opportunity to return to Judea as an act of divine liberation and redemption. The Exodus story became central to the biblical collection because it resonated with the experience of the biblical authors and redactors.[1] Like so many of us, they saw themselves *k'ilu* ("as though") they were freed from the land of Egypt.

The story of oppression and liberation has resonated deeply with the lived experience of successive generations of Jews. As an ethnic and religious minority, Jews were subject to prejudice, structural oppression, and violence, especially during times of larger social and economic upheaval and stress. Within Christian societies, the possibility of Jewish oppression was exacerbated by the complicated and critical status of Jews as the essential "other" within Christian identity. The list of oppressions is familiar: the Crusades, the Inquisition, and pogroms culminating in the horrors of the Shoah. These historical experiences make the assertion that "we were slaves in the land of Egypt" feel very, very true for many Jews. For African-American Jews whose ancestors were enslaved in America, the assertion that "we were slaves in the land of Egypt" testifies to that more recent historical experience of enslavement.

However, the myth doesn't just say "we were slaves in the land of Egypt"; it also says "God redeemed us from slavery." The identity that we assume is not just one of slaves or former slaves, but slaves redeemed by God. Within the context of the Sinai narrative, God's assertion "I the Eternal am your God who brought you out of the land of Egypt, the house of bondage" (Exodus 20:2) probably functions as what historians of the ancient Near East call the "historical preamble" to the covenant between God and Israel. Historians have long recognized the parallels between the covenant between God and Israel in Exodus and Deuteronomy on the one hand, and ancient Near Eastern treaties between suzerains and vassals (rulers of empires and local kings who are subject to them) on the other. These parallels suggest that this suzerain-vassal relationship served as a model or analogy for the relationship between God and Israel for many biblical authors. Within this treaty model, the assertion that God took Israel out of Egypt sets the ground for obligation. The suzerain (God) says, "I did this for you, so you owe me gratitude and allegiance that will be demonstrated through following my laws and doing my will." In addition, the Exodus story testifies to God's tremendous power that will be deployed on behalf of Israel if Israel obeys the terms of the covenant, but will be deployed against them if they disobey. God brought us out of Egypt not solely because God is a source of liberation but because, as it says in Numbers 15:41, which becomes part of the *Sh'ma*, "I the Eternal am your God, who brought you out of the land of Egypt to be your God: I, the Eternal your God." God brought us out of the land of Egypt to be our God, so that we would be subject to the divine will. Within the biblical narrative, the assertion "I the Eternal am your God who brought you out of the land of Egypt" lays the groundwork for the gratitude and fear that will motivate the acceptance of, and compliance with, the covenant.

Even for Jews who do not understand themselves to be in a covenantal relationship with God, our identity as freed slaves evokes a sense of obligation. The reminder that we were slaves in the land of Egypt has served as a goad and rallying cry for Jewish social justice work for many contemporary Jews. Within the Torah, the reminder that we were slaves or strangers in the land of Egypt is motivation for the fair treatment of the socially and economically vulnerable; Exodus 22:20 states, "You shall not wrong nor oppress a stranger, for you were strangers in the land of Egypt." This connection has been central to much progressive Jewish political action in the United States, especially since World War II. Many American Jews have understood our own collective historical experience of oppression as a motivation for social justice work. We ground our commitments to justice work both in empathy for oppressed people and in gratitude for our recent security, power, and influence in American society. For many contemporary American Jews, social justice work is a way both to "pay it forward" and to use the power that comes from our freedom to work for greater justice in American society.

Thanks to the insights of many scholars and professionals working in the multidisciplinary field of trauma studies, we are now engaging more deeply with the complexities of our assumed identity of former slaves. Collective trauma, like the Shoah, leaves complex footprints. On the one hand, our antennae are attuned to the experiences of vulnerable people in our societies, and our legacy of oppression motivates us to use the power and privilege that we have to work for greater justice. At the same time, we know that the experience of oppression can foster other tendencies. We know that experiences of trauma often lead to chronic feelings of unsafety and difficulty in accurately assessing risk. Recently, scholars and practitioners who study contemporary Jewish identity through the lens of trauma studies have been exploring the impact of our recent communal trauma: not only in the form of Jewish commitments to social justice, but also on Jewish responses to antisemitism, Jewish concerns about intermarriage, and Jewish attitudes toward Israel and Palestine.[2]

For these scholars and practitioners, the biblical exhortations to remember that we were strangers in the land of Egypt in the context of mandates about the treatment of the stranger in our midst assume a different tone. They are not only inspirational calls to empathy, but they are also cautions. They say to us: your imaginary experiences of having been strangers may prime you to oppress the stranger. We, in particular, need to be vigilant about not oppressing the stranger, precisely because we were strangers in the land of Egypt. Nehama Leibowitz sees these two possibilities already reflected in Rashi's commentary on the two different expressions in Exodus 22:20, "You shall not wrong nor oppress a stranger, for you were strangers in the land of Egypt," and Exodus 23:9, "You shall not oppress a stranger, for you know the feelings of the stranger, having yourselves been strangers in the land of Egypt."[3] Rashi reads the first formulation as a warning against treating the vulnerable as we ourselves were treated: "If you wrong him, he can wrong you back and say to you: You also come from strangers. Pot, do not call the kettle black." The second formulation, Rashi reads as an acknowledgment of empathy: "You know the feelings of a stranger, how painful it is for him when you oppress him." If our goal is to respond to the mandate "do not oppress the stranger," the repeated assertion that we were strangers in the land of Egypt can be doubly powerful: calling on the empathy of identification, and calling for vigilance about the unconscious tendencies toward oppression that our assumed identity as former slaves may engender.

The similarity between actual Jewish collective historical experiences and the story of our slavery in Egypt is certainly one reason for the story's sticking power. However, there is also a mystical tradition of interpretation that articulates a compelling resonance between the Exodus story and the drama of our souls' relationship with the Divine. Within this tradition, slavery (or exile) in Egypt is a metaphor for the times when we are unable to perceive the Divine within and around us. We are so alienated from the Divine Presence that we don't even know what we are missing. Within this schema, the Exodus serves as a metaphor for the awakening of our awareness of the Divine and the awakening of our desire to be more connected to God. In this framework, God's statement "I the Eternal am your God who brought you out of the land of Egypt, the house of bondage" points to the newly awakened awareness that allows us to desire and work toward greater connection to the Divine. In the great Chasidic work the *S'fat Emet* (*Language of Truth*), Rabbi Yehudah Leib Alter of Ger writes (and translator Arthur Green interprets), "Love is really the gift of God. This is the meaning of [the verse]: 'I am the Lord your God' [God Himself is the source of your ability to love God]."[4]

Within this understanding of slavery in Egypt, the movement from slavery to freedom is not a one-time event or even an episodic one. It is an ongoing and perennial cycle. As humans, we move through times when the world feels like Egypt: we feel powerless, we are suffering, and we feel alienated from that which is nourishing and life-giving in ourselves and the world around us. At other times, we experience a momentary awareness of the holy—in whatever form that might take for us—that allows us to seek out and connect with this holiness in ourselves, in others, or in the natural world. Even if we have never heard it articulated explicitly, I think the sticking power of the Exodus story is grounded in its resonance with this reality. Regardless of our historical proximity to experiences of political and social oppression, regardless of our degree of power and privilege, we have all experienced this kind of Egypt and, hopefully, this kind of redemption.

For the Chasidim, the relationship between the Exodus and Sinai, which is emphasized by the placement of our verse at the head of the Ten Commandments, is this: The Exodus awakens in us the awareness and hunger for deeper relationship with the Divine. Torah, as symbolized by the Ten Commandments, provides the road map for deepening that relationship, for making us more aware of the will of God as it is expressed within us and around us, and for helping us align our actions and our lives as expressions of that holiness within us.

For millennia, Jews have held differing opinions on what it means to live in accordance with God's will or in alignment with the Divine. The subsequent essays in this collection will explore the way in which the Ten Commandments have been crucial texts in this conversation and how they have served as grounding for, and expression of, Jewish ethical commitments and convictions over the centuries. Our verse "I the Eternal am your God who brought you out of the land of Egypt, the house of bondage" doesn't answer the question "What does God want?" or "How do we live in alignment with the holy?" However, it exhorts us to understand God as the source of our liberation, both collective and individual, and to use our freedom and our power as free people in ways that reflect and honor the holiness at its source.

NOTES

1   Peter Machinist, "Outsiders or Insiders: The Biblical View of Emergent Israel and Its Contexts," in *The Other in Jewish Thought: Constructions of Jewish Culture and Identity*, ed. L. Silberstein and R. Cohn (New York: New York University Press, 1993), 35–60.

2   Tirzah Firestone, *Wounds into Wisdom* (Rhinebeck: Adam Kadmon Books, 2019).

3   Nehama Leibowitz, *Studies in Shemot* (Jerusalem: World Zionist Organization, 1983).

4   Yehudah Leib Alter of Ger, *The Language of Truth: The Torah Commentary of the Sefat Emet*, trans. and interpreted by Arthur Green (Philadelphia: Jewish Publication Society, 1998), 330.

Second Commandment

לֹא יִהְיֶה־לְךָ אֱלֹהִים אֲחֵרִים עַל־פָּנָי׃
לֹא תַעֲשֶׂה־לְךָ פֶסֶל וְכָל־תְּמוּנָה אֲשֶׁר
בַּשָּׁמַיִם מִמַּעַל וַאֲשֶׁר בָּאָרֶץ מִתַּחַת וַאֲשֶׁר
בַּמַּיִם מִתַּחַת לָאָרֶץ׃ לֹא־תִשְׁתַּחֲוֶה לָהֶם
וְלֹא תָעָבְדֵם כִּי אָנֹכִי יהוה אֱלֹהֶיךָ אֵל
קַנָּא פֹּקֵד עֲוֺן אָבֹת עַל־בָּנִים עַל־שִׁלֵּשִׁים
וְעַל־רִבֵּעִים לְשֹׂנְאָי׃ וְעֹשֶׂה חֶסֶד לַאֲלָפִים
לְאֹהֲבַי וּלְשֹׁמְרֵי מִצְוֹתָי׃

*You shall have no other gods besides Me. You
shall not make for yourself a sculptured image,
or any likeness of what is in the heavens above,
or on the earth below, or in the waters under
the earth. You shall not bow down to them or
serve them. For I the Eternal your God am
an impassioned God, visiting the guilt of the
parents upon the children, upon the third and
upon the fourth generations of those who reject
Me, but showing kindness to the thousandth
generation of those who love Me and keep My
commandments.*

—Exodus 20:3–6

Prohibition of Idolatry

Rabbi Reuven Firestone, PhD

IN 1917, RUDOLF OTTO published a book entitled *Das Heilige*, "The Holy,"[1] in which he argued for the first time in modern scholarly language that powerful religious experience (what he called "the Holy") is an irrational feeling that is "wholly other" (*das ganz Andere*), entirely different from anything we could possibly encounter in ordinary life, an "experience of both terror and awe" (in Latin: *mysterium tremendum et fascinans*). To Otto, the Holy is both terrifying (*tremendum*) and fascinating (*fascinans*), overwhelmingly powerful but also merciful and gracious.

While Otto's book was one of the most influential studies in the academic study of religion of the twentieth century, Jewish tradition had already been grappling with "*das Heilige*" for thousands of years. In I Kings 19:11–13 for example (in a reprise of Exodus 33:19–23), God passes before the prophet Elijah in a show of both *tremendum* and *fascinans*: "a wind so strong that it was splitting mountains and breaking rocks in pieces," and an earthquake and fire and, finally, "a sound of sheer silence" (*kol d'mamah dakah*).[2] The I Kings text makes clear that God was "not in the wind . . . not in the earthquake . . . [and] not in the fire," but it does not say that God was not in the "sound of sheer silence."

Wherever and however God's divineness is manifest, it can be expressed only indirectly. We cannot really make sense of it, so we try through methods like metaphor—"not in the wind, not in the earthquake." The utter transcendence of God has always been for Jews a *mysterium*. And yet, God must somehow be experienced in a way that can be sensed or imagined—directly or indirectly—through the senses and through our imagination. Through language, art, and any way that we can express our consciousness of the transcendent, we try to make sense of the extraordinary essence and nature of what cannot really be made sense of.

The word for holy in Hebrew is *kadosh* (קָדוֹשׁ), which at its core means something that is "apart" or "other," somehow separate from anything that is ordinary. However, there is no way to convey the inexpressibleness of the Divine except through images that we *can* express and notions with which we *are* familiar. In other words, we can only express the extraordinary through means of the ordinary. Because we cannot avoid using familiar images to convey the extraordinary, our very attempt to make sense of it renders it in some way ordinary. That can easily lead to something that might be considered idolatry.

Another twentieth-century scholar of religion, Mircea Eliade, writes of what he called *hierophany*, "manifestation of the sacred." His word *hierophany* comes from the Greek *hieros*, "sacred," and *phainein*, "reveal, bring to light"—bringing to light the holy.[3] The absolutely transcendent can be manifest in the beauty or extraordinary nature of the familiar: the magnificence of a massive tree or mountain, or the exquisiteness of a flower or a spring of clear bubbling water. Jewish texts are familiar with such manifestations of transcendence, from the fiery sparkle of a desert tree that seems to be on fire (Exodus 3:2) to the vitalizing refreshment of cool water flowing from a spring in the desert (e.g., Genesis 16:7–14; Exodus 17:3–4). Those striking phenomena are not sacred in and of themselves, but seem to allude to something marvelous and extraordinary that must have been the source of their creation, the cause of their existence. The problem is that it is easy to confuse the product with the producer; that which is made with its maker. This mixing together is a form of confusion that comes close to idolatry.

It is easy and common to confuse the created with the creator, and it happens in three different ways.

- It happens when we attempt to make sense of the inexpressible otherness of the Divine in the mundane language of daily life.
- It happens when we associate the extraordinary nature of the remarkable with the essence that made it.
- It happens when we desire to be intimate with an essence that is so extraordinary that it seems absolutely other and beyond our reach, while we attempt to hold on to the ordinary.

Any of these can lead to actions or ideas that smack of idolatry.

The biblical commandment in Exodus 20:3–6 prohibiting idolatry lays out three aspects of prohibition:

- "You shall have no other gods besides Me." This indicates that we may not accept the possibility of any divine power other than God.
- "You shall not make for yourself a sculptured image, or any likeness of what is in the heavens above, or on the earth below, or in the waters under the earth." This forbids the creation of any kind of physical representation of God or of anything that might be associated with the Divinity.
- "You shall not bow down to them or serve them." This bans the veneration of such humanly created objects.[4] These three prohibitions are followed by the words "For I the Eternal your God am an impassioned God." The word translated as "impassioned" is *kana* (קַנָּא), which can also be understood as "zealous" or even "jealous." God insists on being the exclusive object of worship.

Here again, we are stuck with the problem of language, for it would be ironic to imagine God "jealous." That emotion seems to be so human. It is a reflection of insecurity and frailty. No one truly powerful would be jealous of others' judgment. How much more ridiculous would such an emotion seem when associated with God?

It seems strange, especially given the preceding, that God is described and represented in the Hebrew Bible in highly anthropo-morphic ways. But there seems to be no alternative. We want to relate to God but are deeply constrained by the limits of human expression. Consequently, God is often depicted in the *Tanach* like a person. God can become angry and jealous, can strike with the hand, can see, and can be angry. God can also love, regret, and be sad.

"Idolatry" is depicted in the Ten Commandments and elsewhere in the Bible in highly human language. It is a transgression against what is proper in terms of *human* interpersonal relationships. Idol-atry is "disloyalty," "betrayal," "infidelity." The prophet Hosea often uses the metaphor of the disloyal spouse to describe the hurt and rage that result from such betrayal.[5]

In the ancient world of the Near East, the difficulty of being loyal to the one great God was real. Israel was the only community whose theology was absolutely unary. And here we encounter another problem with language: in the *Tanach*, it is the "God of the entire universe" who is associated with the "God of Israel." This associa-tion of absolute universal power with a single community must have seemed absurd. How could a relatively small community of people such as Israel have the audacity to consider the great God of all to be its "own" deity?

To this question, at least, there is a likely answer. In the environ-ment of the ancient Near East in which the Israelites became an identifiable community, it was understood universally that nature was governed by sentient powers that provided rain, brought the sun daily, ensured that crops and animals were fertile, etc. In addition to the deities that governed nature, every distinct population had its own community deity, many of which we know from the Bible. The god of Israel's Ammonite neighbors to the east was known as Milkom (I Kings 11:5), the god of the Moabites to the southeast was Kemosh (Numbers 21:29), the Philistines to the west had a god named Dagon (I Samuel 5), and so on. Virtually every sovereign community had its own god and was probably identified by its unique relationship with it. The Moabites, for example, who worshiped Kemosh, are referred to as "Mo'av . . . the People of Kemosh" (Numbers 21:29), and the community deity of Shechem (today's Nablus) was known as "God of the Covenant" (*El-B'rit*; Judges 9:46), which probably reflects a sense of exclusive relationship between the Shechemites and their god, paralleling the covenant between God and Israel. In the earliest period of Israelite history, Israel also had its own, exclusive community god, which was understood not as the God of all Creation, but rather as a limited tribal god like all the others. For some reason that remains unknown, the Israelites over many generations arrived at the understanding that one great God created the entire universe. It was natural for them to associate that great creator god with their own tribal god, the god they knew so well. Thus, the God of Israel eventually came to be understood as the God of the universe. Given this historical development, it is easy to explain the frequent biblical use of anthropomorphic terms when referring to God.[6]

True loyalty to the one great God meant denying the existence of all the many divine powers that were worshiped by Israel's neighbors. According to virtually everyone else, the world was sustained by powerful deities that, despite their power to bring rain or cause crops and herds to be fertile, were not all-powerful and all-knowing. In such a cultural environment, one might truly wish to be loyal to God, but it would be tempting to "hedge one's bets" and make offerings to other gods in the neighborhood as well. This tendency to "cheat" on the God of Israel by worshiping other deities plagued the Israelites for centuries. One revealing section of the *Tanach* describes rampant idol worship practiced in Jerusalem many generations after Kings David and Solomon, even within the Temple precinct, which was finally eliminated by King Josiah in the seventh century BCE (II Kings 23:4–15).

There is another aspect to the biblical prohibition of idolatry: the prohibition against making any kind of image that is used to represent the true God. Not only must one remain faithful to the one true God, one must not represent the true God improperly.

Some thinkers have noted that the Bible does allow God to be represented in quite striking anthropomorphic imagery, but only through words and not through images.[7] This may be a response to the common practice of physical representation of deities among Israel's neighbors, something that, if practiced by Israel, could lead to venerating the images of other deities as well.

By the middle of the Second Temple period, some centuries after King Josiah, monotheism had become widely known and respected in Judea and its environs even among non-monotheists. By then, Jews felt little pressure to "stray after other gods." By that time, Greek cultural influence had introduced a new kind of philosophical thinking about God, which strove to articulate a reasonable metaphysical understanding of divinity. In the wake of this new way of thinking, people began to believe that they had to formulate for themselves a reasonable or "proper" conception of God. Improper or erroneous formulations could be considered transgressive, even idolatrous. A connection then developed between theological error and idolatry. If you don't understand God "correctly," you are essentially an idolater. This association between "wrong theology" and idolatry became central for Christianity and later also for Islam, but it echoed to a certain extent in some expressions of Judaism as well.

One result of this inclination to equate theological error with idolatry can be found in the current claim of some popular atheists that all religion is false—and thus a form of idolatry. If God does not exist, then the veneration of God in any manner is idol worship, a twist of Jeremiah 16:20: "Can a person make gods for oneself? No-gods are they!"

This self-assured, arrogant expression of atheism overlooks the transcendent *Heilige* of Rudolf Otto and Eliade's manifestation of the sacred that we can often feel lying beneath and behind the awesome and the beautiful—and if we allow it, even the ordinary. Rabbi Abraham Joshua Heschel may have said it in the most intimate way when he taught that we are best able to "see" God when we can allow ourselves to be open to the "radical amazement" in relation to the world around us. "Awe . . . is the sense of wonder and humility inspired by the sublime or felt in the presence of mystery."[8] "Awe enables us to perceive in the world intimations of the divine, to sense in small things the beginning of infinite significance, to sense the ultimate in the common and the simple; to feel in the rush of the passing the stillness of the eternal."[9]

Notes

1   It was translated into English as *The Idea of the Holy: An Inquiry into the Non-Rational Factor in the Idea of the Divine and Its Relation to the Rational*, trans. John Harvey (London: Oxford University, 1923).

2   NRSV translation. Or, perhaps "a sound of near silence." It was classically translated as a "still small voice." For a full discussion, see Havilah Dharam-raj, "A Prophet Like Moses? A Narrative-Theological Reading of the Elijah Narratives" (Durham University thesis, 2006), 80–104, http://etheses.dur.ac.uk/2666/1/2666_678.pdf.

3   Mircea Eliade, *The Sacred and the Profane* (New York: Harcourt Brace Jovanovich, 1957).

4   It is interesting to note that there is no prohibition here against worshiping natural phenomena as representing the Divine, as is common in many traditional native religious practices. In native religion, the natural phenomena may represent a separate power or may represent aspects or attributes of a great single power over all of nature.

5   The image begins already in Hosea 1:2, and it echoes earlier material associating the worship of other deities with whoring or prostituting (Deuteronomy 31:16, where Israel will "go astray after the alien gods"; Judges 2:17, where Israel "did not obey their chieftains but went astray after other gods").

6   Mark S. Smith, *The Origins of Biblical Monotheism* (Oxford: Oxford University, 2001); Smith, *The Early History of God: Yahweh and the Other Deities in Ancient Israel* (Dearborn, MI: Eerdmans, 2002); Ziony Zevit, *The Religions of Ancient Israel: A Synthesis of Parallactic Approaches* (London: Continuum, 2001); Nili Fox, "Concepts of God in Israel and the Question of Monotheism," in *Text, Artifact, and Image: Revealing Ancient Israelite Religion*, ed. G. Berkman and T. Lewis (Atlanta: SBL Brown Judaic Studies, 2006), 326–45.

7   See Moshe Halbertal and Avishai Margalit, *Idolatry* (Cambridge, MA: Harvard University Press, 1992).

8   Abraham Joshua Heschel, *God in Search of Man* (New York: Farrar, Straus and Giroux, 1955 [repr. 1983]), 77.

9   Heschel, *God in Search of Man*, 75.

Why the Second Commandment Still Matters

A Conversation with Maimonides

KENNETH SEESKIN, PhD

THE SECOND COMMANDMENT as presented at Exodus 20:4–6 reads as follows:

> You shall not make for yourself a sculptured image, or any like-
> ness of what is in the heavens above, or on the earth below, or
> in the waters under the earth. You shall not bow down to them
> or serve them. For I the Eternal your God am an impassioned
> God, visiting the guilt of the parents upon the children, upon
> the third and upon the fourth generations of those who reject
> Me, but showing kindness to the thousandth generation of
> those who love Me and keep My commandments.

Two reasons why this commandment is noteworthy come to my mind immediately.

First, it is the only one of the Ten Commandments that makes explicit mention of guilt and punishment. God is so serious about preventing idol worship that God is willing to punish the great- and great-great-grandchildren of those who engage in it. Although this may seem unfair to us, in the ancient world it was not uncommon for punishments to extend over more than one generation. God slays the firstborn Egyptian children to punish Pharaoh. The Israelites are commanded to destroy the remnants of the Amalekites for what their ancestors did during the Exodus. Eventually the idea that God might punish succeeding generations for the sins of their parents was rejected by the prophets Jeremiah (31:29) and Ezekiel (18:1–4), as well as by later Rabbinic commentators. The original meaning of the biblical sentence ceased to be a part of Jewish theology. Still, the seriousness with which God presents this commandment cannot be overstated. That raises a key question: What is so bad about bowing down to an idol?

The second noteworthy feature is that despite God's warning about disobedience, it is not clear what the rationale for this commandment is. Whatever it is, it does not seem possible to arrive at it through common sense only. The prohibitions against murder, stealing, and false witness appear to have basic social functions: they ensure that we all might live together relatively peacefully. Any society that allowed them to be abolished would soon perish. The commandment of keeping Shabbat comes with a justification: we should rest on the seventh day because God rested. The commandment of honoring one's parents also appears to have basic social functions: it ensures both parenthood and old age in dignity. But why are we prevented from making images of God? Almost every other nation in the ancient world did, and many of them, such as Greece and Rome, flourished both artistically and intellectually. Along these lines, it is noteworthy that Exodus 24:10 says quite clearly that Moses and the elders of Israel *saw* God. Similar sentiments are expressed by Isaiah (6:1) and Ezekiel (1:26–28). In the latter case, Ezekiel says that he saw God in human form.

So why not us? What is the reason behind God's prohibition and the seriousness with which it is delivered?

Two explanations suggest themselves. The first is that while it may be technically possible to make an image of God, *that is not how God wants to be worshiped.*[1] This makes the second commandment a matter of divine preference. Although the other nations do things one way, because Israel is called on to be a special nation, it must do things a different way. In short, it is not that one *cannot* see God; merely that Jews *should not* use an image of God as the basis of their worship.

The second explanation for the commandment goes further: actually, *God cannot be seen and therefore cannot be represented in any form whatever*. In support of this view, Deuteronomy 4:12 says that while the people heard a voice at Mount Sinai, they saw no form. On this account, the second commandment is a matter not of preference but of metaphysical necessity: some things cannot be represented by visual images.

As one might expect, the philosophical tradition as exemplified by Maimonides came down on the side of the second option. For Maimonides, anything that can be seen or imagined—that is, anything material—occupies space. Because space is divisible, anything that occupies space must be divisible as well. Anything that is divisible is composed of pieces or parts. Anything that is composed of pieces or parts owes its existence to an external force responsible for putting the parts together—a carpenter, an automaker, a brick layer, or in the case of animals, a mother and father. It follows that if God occupies space and can be seen, then God must owe his or her existence to a superior being, which is absurd. Therefore, God is not composed of pieces or parts, and any attempt to create an image of God in wood or stone misrepresents the nature of God's existence. If the people saw no form at Sinai, it is because God has no form.

There is a tension between Maimonides's argumentation and the biblical texts speaking about God's visual appearance. As we saw, some passages seem to say that God can be seen. It is entirely possible that when Exodus 40:34 says that the glory (*kavod*) of God filled the Tabernacle, people in the ancient world thought that God did occupy space. While it may be difficult to represent a cloud in wood or stone, it is not impossible. Nonetheless it is fair to say that eventually the Deuteronomic view, which suggests that God has no form, came to predominate. In other words, Maimonides's view won out.

It is not uncommon for historians of the ancient Near East to object that the prohibition against idolatry misses an important point. Pagan peoples like the Greeks and Romans were not so ignorant as to think that the statues they bowed down to were identical with the actual gods themselves. For example, Zeus was supposed to reside on Mount Olympus, but representations of him (statues and drawings) could be found throughout the Greek world. In a similar way, the ruler of a country may be represented in pictures or statues erected in public places. Although the ruler might insist that people show respect for these pictures or statues, no one thinks that the ruler inhabits them. Rather, they are substitutes for the ruler, who can be in only one place at a time. To honor the image is to honor the ruler; to dishonor the image is to dishonor the ruler. What, then, is wrong with saying that while God cannot be seen, pictures or statues of God could serve as physical manifestations of God?

The answer is that when a statue stands for something, there is usually a visual resemblance between the original and the thing that represents it. It is no accident that statues of Zeus depicted a man with a muscular torso and a strong, serious expression. Aphrodite, the goddess of love, had wavy hair and a gorgeous figure. Ares, the god of war, is usually seen with a weapon and battle helmet. Marduk, the patron god of Babylon, was depicted as a snake dragon. Asherah, the mother goddess, had protruding breasts. All of these representations were intended to tell us something about the deity and to inspire fear, courage, or sexual attachment.

Suppose, however, that someone were to say that these depictions are way off the mark. Divinity has nothing to do with muscles, breasts, or snakes. The God who called Israel to service is interested in just treatment of the poor and the sick, mercy and forgiveness for those who turn to God in a spirit of repentance, honesty in dealings with other people, and love of one's neighbor.

No muscle-bound man or voluptuous woman, no snake, sea monster, or heavenly creature can depict these ideas. No matter how fearful or attractive, they would only detract from what God wants of us. That is why Deuteronomy 4:12 says that when they received the Ten Commandments at Sinai, the people heard a voice but saw no form. The voice is the call of duty: here are the terms of the covenant between God and Israel. A form—*any* form—would obscure the nature of the divine-human relationship by introducing extraneous factors.

Let us grant that historically, pictures and statues of God were objectionable. But, some might say, idols have gone the way of swords and shields. Not even the most wayward Jew bows down to such things or brings sacrifices to them. If so, why do we need the second commandment today? Though it may have been important in times past, what possible relevance does it have for us?

In answer to this question, those who followed in the Maimonidean tradition extended the second commandment to include not only the prohibition against worshiping pictures or statues, but also the images that one forms in one's mind. In other words, if one prays to God while imagining a man sitting on a throne or a woman behind a judicial bench, one is guilty of idolatry no matter how sincere the prayer may be. Along these lines, Maimonides went so far as to equate the imagination with the evil impulse (*yetzer hara*), the ultimate source of sin.[2] His point was that, however lively, the imagination is still restricted to images of material things that occupy space—either real or make-believe. To conjure up any kind of image of God in one's mind is therefore to make the same mistake as erecting a statue.

Maimonides was also aware that the need to think in spatial terms, to make everything concrete, is a powerful force in human life no matter what century we are talking about. Simply put: our imagination lures us into thinking that only things that occupy space are real. His response was to say that as powerful as the need to concretize things may be, the second commandment asks us to resist it. We could not do physics, higher mathematics, moral theory, jurisprudence, or human psychology if we relied on the imagination alone. In view of this, it is no surprise that Maimonides recommended the study of physics and mathematics as a way of preparing for the study of God; he thought they would free the mind from its attachment to material things.[3]

Let us suppose that we could represent God by forming an image in our minds. Would it be a man or a woman? Would the skin tone be white, brown, or black? Would the figure be tall or short? Would the person be young or old? Would the facial expression be stern or relaxed? As we saw with muscles and breasts, all of these miss the point.

In most cases, the images that emerged would probably reflect our own facial characteristics, skin colors, and body types—meaning that if we prayed while producing these mental images, for all intents and purposes, we would be praying to our own image! As the sixth-century BCE Greek philosopher Xenophanes put it, the Ethiopians say their gods are snub-nosed and have black skin, the Thracians that their gods have blue eyes and red hair, and if horses and oxen could draw pictures, their gods would look remarkably like horses and oxen.

It should now be clear why God insisted on obedience to the second commandment in such strong terms. While the second commandment prohibits statues and pictures of God, it does not prohibit all forms of artistic representation.[4] In Exodus 31:1-11, God calls on Bezalel, whom God has "endowed . . . with a divine spirit," to oversee the artistic designs that will go into the making of the Tabernacle. Inside the Tabernacle, the Ark of the Covenant had statues of two figures (*cherubim*) on top of it. Nothing in the second commandment prohibits non-representational designs, nor does it prohibit images of animals such as lions or plants being affixed to the Ark or religious implements. The *Shulchan Aruch*, a sixteenth-century legal code, prohibits three-dimensional images that could lead to worship and even two-dimensional images of complete human bodies, angels, or heavenly bodies except for purposes of religious, medical, or scientific study. The rationale is that these things could easily take the place of idols.[5]

Underlying all this is the conviction that only God as an abstract concept can be worshiped and that anything that presents itself as a substitute for or a physical representation of God is objectionable. While the specifics of which images are allowed and which ones are forbidden may not be applied with the same degree of rigor across all the denominations of Judaism, if the religion we practice is to promote a particularly humble way of looking at the world and our place in it, then the second commandment and its call to encounter God without creating a visual representation is as valid today as it was at the beginning of our story.

Notes

1   For a detailed account of the various ways that idolatry has been understood, see Moshe Halbertal and Avishai Margalit, *Idolatry* (Cambridge, MA: Harvard University Press, 1992), especially chapter 2.

2   See Maimonides, *Guide of the Perplexed* 2:12.

3   Maimonides, *Guide of the Perplexed* 1:34.

4   For a systematic account on the Jewish position on artistic representation, see Steven S. Schwarzschild, "The Legal Foundation of Jewish Aesthetics," in *The Pursuit of the Ideal*, ed. Menachem Kellner (Albany: State University of New York Press, 1990), 109–16.

5   *Shulchan Aruch, Yoreh De'ah*, 141:4–6.

THIRD COMMANDMENT

לֹא תִשָּׂא אֶת־שֵׁם־יהוה אֱלֹהֶיךָ לַשָּׁוְא כִּי
לֹא יְנַקֶּה יהוה אֵת אֲשֶׁר־יִשָּׂא אֶת־שְׁמוֹ
לַשָּׁוְא:

*You shall not swear falsely by the name of the
Eternal your God; for the Eternal will not clear
one who swears falsely by God's name.*

—Exodus 20:7

The Mystical Experience
of the Divine Name

RABBI MORDECAI FINLEY, PhD

THIS ESSAY is a guided introduction into a particular practice of Jewish mysticism: the mystical experience of the divine name (*YHVH*). The practice I will teach is based on a somewhat detailed map of human consciousness with a specific terminology. The map is crucial for the guidance toward an experience of the divine name.

The Map: A Mystical Terminology

For some people, the map and its terminology interfere with spiritual and mystical experience. For others, like me, the map and its key terms have been a great aid in both spiritual and moral growth as well as a key guide to mystical experience. For many, studying and understanding the map and its terminology is actually the beginning of the experience of the divine name.

I see the mystical experience at the (deep) end of the spectrum of reflective spiritual experiences. I say "reflective" because I am setting aside for the moment spiritual and mystical experiences that might be achieved spontaneously, such as through ecstatic dancing or singing. I am not discounting those practices. My own path—the only one I can teach confidently—has been a much more deliberate contemplative practice. Through such a practice, we can train our consciousness to be receptive to spiritual and mystical experience.

The path that I teach, rooted in Chabad Chasidism, is often called "intellectual" (as Chabad Chasidism is often called in comparison to other Chasidic traditions). If this term connotes "intentional management of consciousness" and "using language to achieve mystical experiences" (as opposed to, for example, chanting by itself), then the term is applied correctly.

The Kabbalah on which Chabad Chasidism is founded teaches that there are ten s'firot ("emanations"), as the Divine Infinite Essence unfolds. These ten s'firot are dynamic and grouped in various ways.[1] The upper s'firot, the "mystical s'firot," can only be experienced through a consciousness devoid of the outside world and even the consciousness of the self. The lower seven s'firot are those whose forces can be readily observed in the Ego Self (as defined below) by means of contemplation. We might call these the "psychological s'firot." The lowest s'firah (Malchut) reflects the state of consciousness when we first look within and witness the fractious state of our inner lives. In general, these lower seven s'firot are understood as having endured a cosmic fracturing in the divine unfolding, called sh'virat hakeilim ("the breaking of the vessels"). The concept of sh'virat hakeilim, one of the hallmarks of Lurianic Kabbalah, is also a foundation of Chabad Chasidism.

In the mystical practice of experiencing the divine name, the letters of the divine name found in the Bible, YHVH, are superimposed on the system of the s'firot. The first s'firah of the mystical group, Keter, is beyond consciousness and will be discussed below. The second s'firah, Chochmah, is labeled with the letter yud. The third s'firah, Binah, is labeled with hei. The middle six s'firot, whose forces are found in the Ego Self, are labeled with vav, and the last s'firah, the experience of human brokenness and the entryway into the Ego Self, is identified as the second hei of YHVH.

In my practice and teaching, mystical experience is achieved by ascending through the lower seven s'firot into the higher ones. This ascending through the s'firot is understood to be not only an ascending through human consciousness into the mystical realm, but also as a repair of the fractured state of the divine name, the YHVH, within each of us.

The path through the s'firot may be broken down into two types of practice. Using Chabad terminology, the first, hitbon'nut ("self-examination"), focuses on the seventh and lowest s'firah (Malchut/

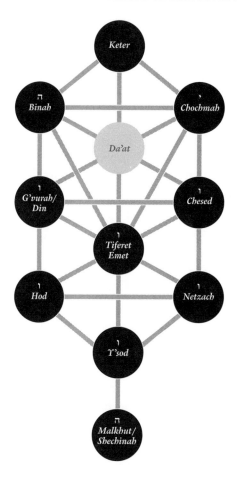

Shechinah). Our consciousness is then guided to rise up into the middle six *s'firot* (*Y'sod*, *Hod*, *Netzach*, *Tiferet*, *G'vurah*, and *Chesed*). The second practice, *hitbod'dut* ("self-isolation" or "self-insulation"), focuses on the mystical experience of the upper *s'firot*, *Binah* and *Chochmah*, and finally, of the highest *s'firah*, *Keter*.

Hitbon'nut ("self-examination") connotes a deliberate reflective or contemplative spiritual practice. *Hitbon'nut* first requires a state of consciousness in which one can "rise" into the Higher Self and examine the contents of the Ego Self. For our purposes, we will call this Higher Self *Daat* ("knowledge"), an aspect of consciousness that mediates between the Ego Self (where the lower seven *s'firot* are experienced) and the mystical consciousness of the upper *s'firot*. Through *hitbon'nut*, I conceive of four aspects of the self (the following are my terms and definitions): the Ego Mind, the Ego Self, the Higher Self (*Daat*), and the Archetypal Self, deep in the subconscious (not to be discussed here).

1. The Ego Mind is our day-to-day consciousness. It takes for granted its own interpretation of the world. The Ego Mind is, however, shaped by the subconscious Ego Self, mentioned above. In the Ego Mind, we are barely aware of the rapid processes within the Ego Self.

2. The Ego Self, subconscious and often fractured, processes our experiences of the world. As it reflects the breakage of divine vessels, the Ego Self contains destructive patterns, bringing havoc to the Ego Mind. Our work is to regulate, manage, and eventually reshape the Ego Self according to some vision of virtue, wisdom, and inner well-being.

3. Through contemplative practice, *hitbon'nut*, we access the higher consciousness of *Daat*. From the perspective of the Higher Self, we can then examine the operations of the potentially destructive Ego Self and work to bring order to the chaos. This is where we begin our work of experiencing and healing the divine name. We each carry our own version of the divine breakage within, and as we repair our own brokenness, we are healing the Divine. As we become our true selves, we are healing the divine name.

The Path: A Mystical Process

In the first stage of *hitbon'nut* (the lower *hei* of the divine name, labeled *Malchut/Shechinah*), a stage that one never leaves behind, we might discover, for example, that we have lived much of our lives somewhat dishonestly, behind a persona unconsciously constructed in the Ego Self. The moment we discover "the mask" can be psychologically devastating. We might realize that much of what we say and believe are just strategies to avoid living in a true and righteous way. As we grow spiritually, the distance between the mask and the true self gets smaller. However, our Ego Self might be a powerful agent in hiding that gap from our consciousness. Experiencing our brokenness is the breakthrough to authenticity, to living truly and righteously. Experiencing the breaking of the mask can be a moment of both extraordinary pain and extraordinary beauty and wholeness. By breaking the mask, we can begin to heal the brokenness. God's love and grace can fill the space that pretenses inhabited. The recognition of our own mask, the experience of its breakage, and our will to become more authentic human beings is to experience the lower *hei* of the divine name, *YHVH*. This experience is the entryway to repairing the divine name.

In our example, through our becoming conscious of wearing a mask and learning how to break it, we can raise our consciousness into the realm of *Daat*. In *Daat*, we loosen the destructive grip of the Ego Self. This work (work we must do all our lives) is the work related to the *vav*, the next letter of the divine name. In the realm of *Daat*, we can consciously and calmly examine the contents of the six *s'firot* of *vav*, the Ego Self, without identifying with them. Along with examining the contents of the Ego Self, *hitbon'nut* also requires a straightening out of bad habits and bad theories. One seeks to be rational and moral. We aim to maximize, for example, love, justice, truth, and beauty. With enough training, the qualities of *Daat* (the Higher Self) will overcome the bad habits of the Ego Self. Centering ourselves in *Daat* can produce, almost as by-products, moments of stillness in which we can discern a quiet Divine Presence guiding us in our work.

I want to stress this: regular deliberate ascension into the realm of *Daat* ("knowledge"), in which we can see and regulate the Ego Self, can be a deeply spiritual, transformative, and even mystical experience. It usually takes several months of practice to be able to ascend to the further reaches of *Daat*, where we can regulate the Ego Self.

For some, that is as far as they want to go. There are some, however, who, upon sensing a Presence in *Daat* that they can't quite name, want to find their way into that Presence. Using the divine name as a guide, they want to move up from the second *hei* and *vav* and go beyond *Daat* into the mystical: the first *hei*, and then the *yud* of *YHVH*.

In order to move into the upper *s'firot*, we practice *hitbod'dut* instead of *hitbon'nut*. As the word in Hebrew suggests, we move into an experience of being "isolated" or "insulated." In *hitbod'dut*, we lose track of any consciousness of the Ego Mind or Ego Self. We are not doing conscious spiritual work. We are ascending into the realm of *Binah*. While *Binah* is usually translated as "discernment," conceptually, *Binah* refers to something like "the ramified point of the origins of consciousness." In *Binah*, we encounter a "presence," *HaMakom*, and we realize that this Presence has always been there, within and without us. Chasidism teaches that love of the Divine generates the will and the pull to ascend into that Presence.

The *hitbod'dut* practice I teach is the contemplation of holy words. Mystical texts suggest that in *Binah*, we "taste" holy words, such as my beloved list of the garments of God: love, justice, truth, and beauty. I have found it helpful to study these terms in religious, spiritual, and philosophical literature. For example, I recall that the Hebrew word for "spirit" or "soul," *n'shamah*, refers to the divine breath that was breathed into the primordial human being. In my own breathing, I meditate on and experience the breath of God within. Many teach that as we breathe in, the Divine breathes out. We breathe out—the Divine breathes in. Sometimes in the midst of that breathing, I chant Proverbs 20:27 in Hebrew, "The light of the Divine is the human soul," rooting my consciousness in each of these words.

In the realm of *Binah*, where we "taste" the meaning of holy words, the tone and contents of our consciousness are transformed. We may feel as if we have entered another world, a world that can be experienced as more real than the physical reality we normally inhabit. One can experience the power of holy words. The holy words replace the drives of the Ego Self.

Our next step takes us into the realm of the purely mystical, into an actually different world—the world of *Chochmah*, the *yud*, the first letter of *YHVH*, "That Which Causes Being." In mystical literature, the *yud/Chochmah* connotes the generative point of consciousness from which all reality proceeds. Our consciousness transcends even our breathing and the tasting of holy words. We connect to the most real world. We realize that we human beings are just a figure of speech of the Divine Presence that spoke reality into being. We are a fleeting breath, emitted from a reality so real that for a moment our consciousness is obliterated, and nothing but divine Nothingness exists.

No language exists in mystical experience—there is no consciousness that can produce language. There is only a riotous silence that can leave you shuddering once you regain your sense of self. We try to use language to name the experience afterward but are limited to failing metaphors. Experiencing the realm of *yud/Chochmah* is to merge consciousness with the Divine Consciousness from which all reality proceeds.

As I mentioned above, *yud/Chochmah* is not the final, highest *s'firah*. Beyond the *yud* is "that which cannot be named." The term *Keter* ("crown," above *Chochmah*) is simply a holding place for "consciousness beyond naming," a mediation into Nothingness. When we consider *Keter*, also called "Nothingness" (*ayin*), "will" (*ratzon*), and "thought" (*machshavah*), we understand that *YHVH* is not the ultimate name of the Divine. In Chabad mystical theory and practice, *YHVH* is understood as referring to the *m'haveh*—"the aspect of the Divine that renders Pure Being into Being." In the realm called *Keter*, we go beyond that which renders Being. We rise into nothing else. One becomes a knower of God, a knower of "the Essence" of "the Nothingness." One knows No Thing. One experiences one's own nonbeing, as one experiences Divine Nonbeing as the root of Divine Being. It is fearsome and it is beautiful. And it can change everything. The echo of Nothingness never leaves us.

In that moment, one might understand that light is the garment of God (Psalm 104:2). When we see light, we see the shape of the Divine. What we see out in the world are shadows of the colors of the prism on a wall, but we can experience the actual colors on the wall if we go within. In our day-to-day consciousness, we can pause and sense the prism that generates the colors, that which renders Pure Being into being. We might shudder.

How does one hold that consciousness? We have to ascend, perhaps daily, into the realm of *Daat*, in which we can both examine and regulate our Ego Self. Sometimes the realm of *Daat*, on its own accord and in its own time, will turn us from examining the contents of the Ego Self, into the mystical realms.

In this work (the contemplating, the ordering of the chaos, the breathing, the tasting of holy words, the inner seeing) we find our true self, authentic life, and purpose of Being.

NOTE

1   It is crucial to note that the labels of the *s'firot* (for example, the upper three: *Keter*, "Crown"; *Chochmah*, "Wisdom"; *Binah*, "Discernment"), do not indicate their conceptual content.

God's Name in Theurgy, Amulets, and Magic Spells

Contemporary Lessons fom Ancient Jewish Magic

Rabbi Geoffrey W. Dennis

PERHAPS IT OCCURS in other parts of the country too, but here in Texas, Jews often experience a momentary confusion, or even a sense of annoyance, when a stranger wishes us, "A blessed day!" We chuckle uneasily when a Jewish acquaintance responds to our casual "How are you?" with a "Thank God!"

Anyone who has had such moments still has the third commandment shaping their thinking.

What is the nature of the third commandment, *Lo tisa et shem Yud-Hei-Vav-Hei Elohecha lashav ki lo y'nakeh Yud-Hei-Vav-Hei eit asher yisa et sh'mo lashav*, "You shall not swear falsely by the name of *Yud-Hei-Vav-Hei* your God; for *Yud-Hei-Vav-Hei* will not clear one who swears falsely by God's name" (Exodus 20:7; Deuteronomy 5:11)?[1] In biblical usage, the word *shem*, "name," is used narrowly to refer a person's name, but also expansively to mean "reputation." Are we simply forbidden to misuse the name of God (from this point forward in this essay, simply "the Name"), or more broadly, are we forbidden to revile or besmirch God in any way? Depending on which early Jewish source one consults, the prohibition can be against one or the other, and in keeping with the usual pattern of how Rabbinic law deals with such controversy, Jewish tradition opts to assume it encompasses both.

One of the implications of the commandment that instructs us to be careful regarding our religious speech is an idea that may be attractive to many contemporary Jews. We generally prefer people to keep their religion private, and the commandment would seem to demand just that. Given that, the third commandment should be a much-cited favorite. Yet despite that, for most of us, the third commandment still presents multiple barriers to appreciating its value.

The first barrier is that *many contemporary Jews no longer readily accept prohibitions, especially when they are related to a concept that seems fundamentally at odds with their worldviews.* On a human-to-God axis, even those who believe in God struggle with the very concept of blasphemy (reviling God). Does God, the Supreme Being, really need legislative protection to secure God's divine reputation against the ill opinion of mere dust and ashes?

Jewish tradition is sensitive to the idea that a supreme being should be so thin-skinned, so it simultaneously honors the existence of the commandment while radically limiting its scope. In *Mishnah Sanhedrin* 7:5, the Rabbis offer a very narrow definition of what it means to insult the Deity: blasphemy is *misusing* the Name, *Yud-Hei-Vav-Hei* (commonly called the Tetragrammaton), the four-letter name of God that appears over a thousand times in the Hebrew Bible. Paradoxically, over time, Jews have expanded the prohibition to cover the unnecessary use of *seven* divine names and titles that appear in the Hebrew Bible: *YHVH, El, Elohim, Shaddai, Tz'vaot, Adonai,* and *Ehyeh Asher Ehyeh.* Still (while we can follow the cautious logic of this tradition), given the supposed power differential between divinity and flesh-and-blood, this seems to be a petty regulation, which presents God as a fragile and defensive deity.

An additional barrier is on the person-to-person axis: *our discomfort with displays of public piety,* as described in the opening paragraph. In contemporary American society, the word "piety" (*chasidut*) has come to be associated with displays of public religiosity, usually associated with certain denominations of Christianity, but also with some Jewish movements. The signal example of this among our Christian neighbors is the increasingly common way to conclude a brief exchange with "Have a blessed day!" Many non-Christian contemporaries recognize this to be an attempt to add a religious

dimension upon what has otherwise been an areligious, even reflex-
ive, exchange of pleasantries. Likewise, the injection of public piety
is often marked by traditional Jews using expressions as "Thank
God!" or, perhaps even more so, the use of the insider expression
HaShem, in place of the commonplace English noun "God": "Thank
HaShem!" or "*Baruch HaShem!*" The written parallel to this is the rel-
atively new custom of refusing to spell out the English nouns "God"
and "Lord," substituting them with the attenuated "G-d" and "L-rd."
The use or non-use of such euphemisms marks the writer as either a
Jewish "insider" or "outsider."

So how can we be true to the liberal values of expansiveness, inclusion, and flexibility while at the same time honoring the appropriate
occasions for us to invoke or call upon God in our public, shared discourse? And how do we know when to adhere to the authentic Jewish
spirit of restraint in addressing God?

While Jewish law based on the third commandment seems mono-
lithic in discouraging the use of God's name under all circumstances,
the actual history of the Name in human hands is much more
complex.

Biblical Sources
In the Hebrew Bible itself, we see an account in which a person is
brutally punished for invoking the Name to curse another (Leviticus 24:10–16), whereas elsewhere we see a prophet curse someone
"in the name of *Yud-Hei-Vav-Hei*" without condemnation (II Kings
2:24). In the *Tanach*, the Hebrew Bible, knowing the Name is por-
trayed as a special gift, granted only to people who enjoy God's favor.
Moreover, it is revealed only under certain circumstances (Exodus
3). Yet, at the same time, God seems to encourage the Israelites to
use the divine name (Isaiah 12:4). Early in the Jewish narrative, God
informs the people of Israel, "In every place where I cause My name
to be remembered, I will come to you and bless you" (Exodus 20:21).
Perhaps most striking of all, while the Torah presents a long list of
forbidden magical practices, there is no prohibition against using
the Name in ritual worship or even in rituals that would strike us as

magical (Exodus 22; Leviticus 19–20; Deuteronomy 18; II Kings
2:24). In a particularly piquant verse, God is said to declare, "is
devoted to Me I will deliver him; I will keep him safe for he knows
My name" (Psalm 91:14). Read literally, this implies that God's name
grants a measure of protection to those who call upon it. Mostly
famously, there is the performative ritual of bestowing the protective
power of the Name through the *Birkat Kohanim*, the Priestly Blessing
(Numbers 6:24–26):

> May *Yud-Hei-Vav-Hei* bless you and guard over you [compare to
> Psalm 121:7];
> May *Yud-Hei-Vav-Hei* cause God's presence to shine upon you
> and be gracious to you;
> May *Yud-Hei-Vav-Hei* look favorably upon you, and grant you
> peace [compare to Leviticus 26:6].
> So they shall put My name on the Children of Israel, and I will
> bless them.

This is a classic example of an adjuration with an imperative tone:
a threefold poetic-magical structure (three words, then five words,
then seven words). That this is an incantation as much as a prayer
(the distinction is very fine indeed) is also evident from the context: the blessing immediately follows a description of a yet another
"magical" ritual—that of the ordeal of the suspected wife, in which
the priests test a woman suspected of infidelity by having her drink a
cursed potion literally made from words of the Torah, including the
Tetragrammaton (Numbers 5:11–31).[2]

So is using God's name for the purposes of protection, divina-
tion, or healing (and sometimes, cursing) actually permitted by the
Tanach?

Many of our ancestors seemed to think so. Despite the impression given by centuries of reticence concerning speaking and writing the Name, Talmudic sources never explicitly declare any limits
on the writing of the Tetragrammaton, though the custom on limiting speaking it aloud is probably quite old. Thus, like the biblical
authors, our Sages did not understand the third commandment to

be a blanket prohibition of writing and speaking the Name. And one does not have to look very far beyond legal traditions to discover that there was a remarkable range of practical uses for the Name: amulets, exorcisms, and healing rituals. In fact, the frequent use of seven of the names of God for beneficent purposes is consistent in the record of Hebrew-language artifacts and texts: magical manuals, protective talismans, mystical teachings, and rituals—all of which extend across continents and centuries.

At the heart of "magical" Jewish rituals that predate the embrace of a scientific worldview is the understanding that it is not only permitted but laudatory to use the Name for the benefit of individuals and the Jewish people as a whole.

In order to understand this perceived utility of God's name, we have to return to the worldview of our ancestors. I already alluded to the idea that it can be deduced from the Bible that the uttering of God's name can be a powerful means to reshape reality. This arises largely from the account of Genesis chapter 1, where God brings the cosmos into being by a series of speech-acts: "Then God said, 'Let there be light,' and there was light" (Genesis 1:3). God's speech is constructive. It makes stuff happen. It should come as no surprise, then, that if our ancestors believed that God's words were powerful, uttering God's name was considered to be powerful, too. They understood the Name to contain the very essence of divine creative power. Further proof of this occurs in *B'reishit Rabbah* 12:10, which interprets Isaiah 26:4 as follows, "For with [the letters] *Yud-Hei*, *Adonai* formed worlds."[3] The Name itself is described to possess some of God's potency.

Perhaps the closest, if somewhat flip modern analogy, is to a PIN code to a bank account.

Using the Name gives us access to the *keren kayemet*, the supernal fund of divine power, caring, and goodness. Further, it is inferred that divine power is meant for humans to use; otherwise, why would God have shared it with us?

Rabbinic and Medieval Sources

Postbiblical traditions extend the biblical logic, creating tales of biblical heroes who make use of God's name, for example Moses[4] and Solomon.[5] Conversely, it gives examples of how access to the Name could be abused by biblical villains.[6]

From late antiquity onward, we see the prolific, if hardly casual, display and application of the Name on Jewish amulets of protection on Hebrew and Aramaic incantation bowls directed against evil spirits in magic squares and magic circles that are rendered through permutation of the vowels into mystical sound poems; as well as visually rearranged so that the four letters mimic the human body in order to activate the Divine Presence within us.

Sefer Chasidim, a book credited to a celebrated thirteenth-century rabbi, Judah the Pious, includes this *maaseh* (rabbinic folktale):

> A rabbi was asked the following question: "A man who has knowledge of the mysteries inherent in God's name, and with this knowledge is able to destroy the enemies of the Jewish people and transform the community into God-fearing Jews, is he permitted to use this mystical power?" Replied the rabbi, "He is allowed to kill the enemy only if he knows with certainty that not one of his enemy's descendants will be a righteous person."[7]

Note that while the use of the Name as a weapon is forbidden without certain knowledge of its future consequences, the consulting rabbi says nothing to discourage its use to "transform the community into God-fearing Jews."

One certainly also finds continuous examples within Jewish traditions of limiting or preventing the use of the Name, most famously by way of euphemisms and substitute words (*Adonai, HaShem, Ado-Shem, HaKadosh Baruch Hu*), part of a regulatory practice well-known and still widely observed, even among liberal and secular Jews. Conversely, as we are about to see, it is equally true that many Jews have felt free to jump over that fence, particularly in matters of well-being, health, and healing.

So even though misuse of the Name has been taboo since the third commandment was penned, that has not meant that its use, *in toto*, has been viewed as evil or in rebellion against the authority of Jewish tradition. Moreover, the adepts who used the Name for good became cultural heroes. In time, demonstrating prowess in using the Name proved so impressive that its attribution to Jewish spiritual heroes became a *sine qua non* in their laudatory biographies. Thus, not only do we read of Talmudic and medieval rabbis who performed celebrated feats using the Name to heal and transform (the *b'nei aliyah y'chidei s'gulah*), but by the end of the medieval period, there was a whole class of shaman-like Jewish healers and ritual performers who came to be known as *baalei HaShem*, "Masters of the Name." Many of us may know of the Baal Shem Tov ("Master of the Good Name"), the founder of the Chasidic movement in the eighteenth century, but few realize this moniker came not from his unique teachings, but from his earlier work as an amulet-maker and faith healer. A more nuanced examination of Jewish tradition, therefore, shows that the Tetragrammaton is not simply a source of "holy dread," but also a sacred tool. The person who says it aloud or writes it can either be engaged in an aggressive or a transgressive-but-awe-inspiring act, working around the nexus of the forbidden and the sacred—just as modern and contemporary Jews have been doing for the past three centuries, as they explore and expand the boundaries of tradition in matters of gender, sex, and cultural relations between Jews and non-Jews.

We may look askance at people who weaponize God's name to assert their moral superiority, to enforce their beliefs, or even to justify violence (this seems to be a clear violation of the third commandment). It is hard, however, to argue against our ancestors, who invoked the Name in public performances and gestures meant to help themselves and their fellow Jews and to advance the well-being of the world. They were part of a mighty stream of biblical, rabbinic, and folk traditions of our people. May we show as much discernment, audacity, and enthusiasm as they did.

NOTES

1   Unless stated otherwise, the translations are the author's own.

2   Maimonides, *Mishneh Torah, Hilchot Sotah* 2. The conditional curse pronounced by the priest is written, in its entirety, including the Name, on a text, which is then allowed to dissolve in a potion the woman is required to drink.

3   Cf. *Babylonian Talmud, M'nachot* 29b.

4   *Sh'mot Rabbah* 1:29.

5   *Babylonian Talmud, Gittin* 68b; *The Testament of Solomon.*

6   *Babylonian Talmud, Sanhedrin* 107b.

7   Yehudah HeChasid, *Sefer Chassidim: The Book of the Pious*, trans. Yaakov Finkel (Northvale, NJ: Jason Aronson, 1997), 115.

Fourth Commandment

זָכוֹר אֶת־יוֹם הַשַּׁבָּת לְקַדְּשׁוֹ: שֵׁשֶׁת יָמִים
תַּעֲבֹד וְעָשִׂיתָ כָּל־מְלַאכְתֶּךָ: וְיוֹם הַשְּׁבִיעִי
שַׁבָּת לַיהוה אֱלֹהֶיךָ לֹא־תַעֲשֶׂה כָל־
מְלָאכָה אַתָּה וּבִנְךָ־וּבִתֶּךָ עַבְדְּךָ וַאֲמָתְךָ
וּבְהֶמְתֶּךָ וְגֵרְךָ אֲשֶׁר בִּשְׁעָרֶיךָ: כִּי שֵׁשֶׁת־
יָמִים עָשָׂה יהוה אֶת־הַשָּׁמַיִם וְאֶת־הָאָרֶץ
אֶת־הַיָּם וְאֶת־כָּל־אֲשֶׁר־בָּם וַיָּנַח בַּיּוֹם
הַשְּׁבִיעִי עַל־כֵּן בֵּרַךְ יהוה אֶת־יוֹם הַשַּׁבָּת
וַיְקַדְּשֵׁהוּ:

Remember the sabbath day and keep it holy.
Six days you shall labor and do all your work,
but the seventh day is a sabbath of the Eternal
your God: you shall not do any work—you,
your son or daughter, your male or female slave,
or your cattle, or the stranger who is within
your settlements. For in six days the Eternal
made heaven and earth and sea—and all that
is in them—and then rested on the seventh day;
therefore the Eternal blessed the sabbath day and
hallowed it.
                                    —Exodus 20:8–11

Permitted and Forbidden Labor
Legal and Ethical Dimensions

RABBI DR. SHMULY YANKLOWITZ

Shabbat and Labor Rights

Shabbat, in the popular imagination, is often framed as a complete submission to piety. One is to desist from work, and in its place to engage in holy rituals (prayers, special meals) and the resistance to engage with worldly affairs. However, at its foundation and its best, Shabbat is to be a powerful vehicle for social justice progress.

Consider the macro-ethic of Shabbat, the cessation of work:

> Remember the sabbath day and keep it holy. Six days you shall labor and do all your work, but the seventh day is a sabbath of the Eternal your God; you shall not do any work—you, your son or daughter, your male or female slave, or your cattle, or the stranger who is within your settlements. For in six days the Eternal made heaven and earth and sea—and all that is in them—and the rested on the seventh day; therefore the Eternal blessed the sabbath day and hallowed it. (Exodus 20:8–11)

Indeed, one may not work one's worker; this is an issue of worker justice. One may not work one's animal; this is an issue of animal welfare. One may not work the land; this is an issue of environmentalism. One may not work oneself; this is an issue of self-care. In contemporary American society, the greatest plague that affects us as a whole is the scourge of rampant materialism; the new idolatry is consumerism. Shabbat is the response, as well as a realigning paradigm to strive for: that once a week, we break free of viewing every person and everything as an instrument for desire. Rather than buy and sell, make and destroy, work and be worked, we rest. We reflect.

It is precisely from the meta-values of Shabbat that an authentic labor ethics emerges. These are not the basic details of labor rights like the right to a living wage, lunch breaks, days off, and being paid overtime. Rather, the enterprise of Shabbat is about developing an existential consciousness that other human beings do not exist to serve our desires. The interruption of economic activity and labor is about developing an egalitarian ethos that fundamentally pushes us toward recognizing the equality of all human beings. The Talmud makes clear that the Creation story reveals a deep truth about human equality:

> [The] first human being was created alone to teach that all who destroy a single life are as though they destroyed an entire universe, and those who save a single life are as if they had saved an entire universe. Furthermore [the first human was created alone] for the sake of peace among people, so that no one could say to another, "My ancestor was greater than yours."[1]

After humans were created, they rested. In the world of work, inequalities will inevitably emerge. But, with Shabbat, we are all equal.

One might think from the biblical verse prohibiting worker oppression that we're only dealing with fellow Jews, since the worker is called our "neighbor," which the Rabbis understand as a Jew:

> You shall not defraud your neighbor. You shall not commit robbery. The wages of a laborer shall not remain with you until morning. (Leviticus 19:13)

But another biblical verse makes clear that this is also true for gentiles:

> You shall not abuse a needy and destitute laborer, whether a fellow Israelite or a stranger in one of the communities of your land. (Deuteronomy 24:14)

The Rabbis explained that worker rights issues may not seem like they are life and death, but should be treated as though they are: "All who withhold an employee's wages, it is as if they have taken their life from him."[2] We learn from the Creation narrative that every human being was created equally in the image of God and that we are responsible for them. Rabbeinu Yonah (thirteenth century, Spain) explains how high the burden of responsibility is if one chooses to take on an employee:

> Be careful not to afflict any living creature, whether animal or bird, and all the more so, one should not afflict a person, who is created in the image of the Divine. If you want to hire laborers and you find that they are poor, they should be [regarded as] poor members of your household, and do not degrade them, for you were commanded to have a respectful manner with them and to pay their wages.[3]

The deep truth that emerges from the Sabbath is that no person can truly be owned by another person. Rather, we all belong to our Creator.

> As it is written, "For it is to Me that the Israelites are servants" (Leviticus 25:55), and not servants to servants.[4]

Our obligations are not just to obey secular law, but to go beyond the letter of the law to ensure that workers are treated with full dignity.[5]

Rabbi Yerucham Levovitz (known as the Mirrer Mashgiach, late nineteenth to early twentieth century, Poland) taught that the name "Noah" (*Noach*) comes from the word *m'nuchah* ("rest"), since Noah was a person concerned with the righteous comfort of the people of his generation. Therefore, embracing *m'nuchah* is an act of emulating God (Genesis 2:2). God created rest and personally enacted it among God's creations.

But what is the nature of this rest? The Shabbat *Minchah* prayer describes the Jewish notion of rest in the following way: "A rest of love and magnanimity, a rest of truth and faith, a rest of peace and serenity and tranquility and security, a perfect rest in which You find favor." Rest is about achieving the deepest of virtues when we are relaxed and focused enough to internalize their truths for the actualization of the soul. And indeed, every person deserves the opportunity for self-actualization. One dimension of self-actualization is made manifest through our social progress in the physical world, including our spiritual actualization achieved in rest. Rabbi Abraham Joshua Heschel (twentieth century, America, originally Poland) explains:

> He who wants to enter the holiness of the day must first lay down the profanity of clattering commerce, of being yoked to toil. He must go away from the screech of dissonant days, from the nervousness and fury of acquisitiveness and the betrayal in embezzling his own life. . . . To set apart one day a week for freedom, a day on which we would not use the instruments which have been so easily turned into weapons of destruction, a day for being with ourselves, a day of detachment from the vulgar, of independence of external obligations, a day on which we stop worshipping the idols of technical civilization, a day on which we use no money . . . is there any institution that holds out a greater hope for man's progress than the Sabbath?[6]

Erich Fromm (twentieth century, philosopher and psychologist, Switzerland, originally Germany) explains that this consciousness must lead to freedom:

> The Sabbath symbolizes a state of union between man and nature and between man and man. By not working—that is to say, by not participating in the process of natural and social change—man is free from the chains of time, although only for one day a week.[7]

Another vital dimension to the Shabbat's inherent dignity is letting go of our mastery of the world. We cultivate humility, knowing that we are not in control and that we submit to the inevitabilities of our frailty and mortality. Rabbi Aryeh Kaplan (twentieth century, America) explains:

> God did not rest because He was tired or overworked. Even creating the universe is not hard work for God. Our Sages teach us that it involved less effort than to pronounce a single letter. God rested in another sense. He rested when he stopped

creating—when He no longer interfered with His world. This gives us an insight into the Torah's definition of Sabbath rest. We rest in a Sabbath sense when we no longer interfere with the world.[8]

We are immersed in responsibilities and commitments to work, family, community, society, and the world. A primary purpose for human existence is to toil, to serve, and to work. The Jewish tradition, overall, places a high priority on the value of work. In *Ethics of the Fathers*, Sh'mayah taught, *Ehav et ham'lachah*, "Love one's occupation."[9] And, Rabbi Shimon ben Elazar said:

> Great is work because even Adam did not taste food until he had performed work, as it is said, "So God Eternal took the man, placing him in the Garden of Eden to work and keep it" (Genesis 2:15). Only then do we read, "God Eternal then commanded the man, saying, 'You may eat all you like of every tree in the garden'" (Genesis 2:16).[10]

Relatedly, commentators argued that the commandment of Shabbat requires not only rest on the seventh day but also work on the previous six days.[11] More recently, Rabbi Joseph B. Soloveitchik (twentieth century, America, originally Russia) argued that human work was at the core of our dignity and sanctified purpose: "When God created the world, He provided an opportunity for the work of His hands—man—to participate in His creation. The Creator, as it were, impaired reality in order that mortal man could repair its flaws and perfect it."[12]

Leisure was once a high priority for Americans. Those who grew up in the post–Second World War period experienced a world of increasing leisure time, usually with a husband making the income and a stay-at-home mom taking care of home and children, and new inventions designed to increase productivity and entertainment in the household.[13]

Yet, by the turn of the millennium, an *ABC News* report noted that "not only are Americans working longer hours than at any time since statistics have been kept, but now they are also working longer than anyone else in the industrialized world."[14]

In the ensuing years, some studies contend that Americans have more leisure time than ever or work less than people in industrializing countries.[15] These studies often use faulty methodology, however, such as assuming that it takes less time to do housework, errands, and other tasks, so there is more time for leisure. This conclusion ignores the additional tasks that have been added to modern housework as a result of living in larger homes with more devices and furniture, longer commutes, an obligation to check work-related text messages and emails at every moment, high competitiveness and stress levels, frequent moves, insecure job situations, and precarious financial setups. Indeed, many Americans do not even take their full amount of annual vacation days (already much fewer than for European workers) for fear that they might lose the "competitive edge."[16] The peak of leisure time was in 1969, when the U.S. Labor Department's American Time Use Survey recorded the most leisure time. Since then, there has been a marked trend toward less leisure time, as the following Harris Poll Table indicates:

AVERAGE WEEKLY LEISURE TIME (Hours)

1973	26
2007	20
2008	16

Regardless of the causes of this trend, there is a consensus that working long hours of overtime is deleterious to one's health. Studies based on data from the Centers for Disease Control and Prevention and the American Psychological Association reveal that workers with the most overtime had

- an increased risk for injury, illness, and mortality, along with poorer perceived general health,
- higher levels of anxiety, depression, and stress, and
- greater interference with their responsibility to family and home.

Conversely, companies that try to balance work and life reap rewards; their employees demonstrate greater innovation, creativity, and productivity and make fewer mistakes. In short, physical and psychological health is enhanced by leisure time.

Thus, one might suggest that rest is not only a Shabbat ethic, but a quotidian necessity. Rabbi Baruch Epstein (nineteenth to twentieth century, Lithuania) argues on this point:

> Consider . . . that for a young man working on Talmudic analysis for five or six hours straight can certainly affect his health . . . and I therefore came upon you at daybreak and told you to go have some tea, and my focus was not the tea but rather the fact that you would have a break. . . . And this, too, I believe, that when one rests in order to reach a certain goal, then that rest is as valuable as the goal itself . . . for the goal of the rest is to add strength and power to the actual pursuing of the goal, whether it be learning or good deeds.[17]

From a Jewish perspective, there is a tendency to value mindful rest more than mindless rest. Taking a break does not mean the primary value is to turn off one's own core faculties, but the opposite. Mindful rest—in which we engage our mind, heart, and soul in different and meaningful ways from the norm—is not only more effective to recharge, but it also ensures that our rest helps promote self-actualization. Maimonides (twelfth century, Egypt, originally Spain) teaches the importance of engaging in pleasures that do not just feel good but strengthen us toward our core goals:

> One should try to achieve through his eating, drinking, intercourse, sleeping, waking, movements, and rests—the goal of his body's health, and the goal of having a healthy body should be that one's soul finds its tools whole and ready to engage in wisdom. . . . And in the same vein one should not be considering only how pleasurable those actions are—which might cause one to choose only that food and drink which tastes good, and so too with the other physical aspects—but rather one should choose that which will be most helpful and effective, whether pleasurable or not.[18]

It is spiritually and morally necessary to see "the fruits of our labor." We are created to work, to change the world for good. But we must not dismiss the religious and ethical value of rest and leisure, for through its responsible actualization, we can truly learn to live fully. Concomitantly, there is a humble dimension to humans (powerless beings that return to the earth), but there is also a majestic dimension (powerful to create change in the world). We must embrace the limits of our work (humility) but also embrace our work to be as effective as possible (majestic). It is not accidental but intentional that our lives should be consumed with labor. Rabbeinu Bachya (thirteenth century, Spain) wrote:

> Humanity's livelihood requires individual's active participation. Apart from the period of (the Israelites') wandering in the wilderness, and other times of miraculous intervention, there is no manna from heaven. This active participation of people in the creation of their own wealth is a sign of spiritual greatness. In this respect we are, as it were, imitators of God.[19]

In addition, Rabbi Joseph B. Soloveitchik taught that there was a fundamental duality to humans:

> The dual religious experience of *majesta* and *humilitas Dei* has had its impact upon Judaic morality. There are . . . two moralities: a morality of majesty and a morality of humility.[20]

The Torah's promise of Shabbat is a subversive revolution reminding us that as important as work is in our lives, rest is a highest aim. Rest does not merely mean fun, but meaningful leisure. Our character can best be assessed by how we choose to use our free time. Does it elevate us and those around us? Does it give us more energy, ideas, and positivity? Does it bring repair to brokenness?

Sadly, many work only to survive. Ideally, every individual would be able to pursue their passions and actualize their unique talents through their work. I truly dream that this is not an impractical ideal, a reality only for the privileged, but that labor can be a vehicle for us all to perfect our souls and the world. It is important that we encourage everyone to experiment with various types of work. We must encourage the upcoming generations to seek out new professional experiences so as to find what they are truly passionate about, and it is imperative that we work to create a more just world where all people can have the ability to seek out the work that best suits them and not merely be forced into a lifetime of unchosen monotonous labor.

Achad HaAm (nineteenth to twentieth century, Palestine, originally Russia) was correct when he wrote, "More than the Jews have kept the Sabbath, the Sabbath has kept the Jews."[21] But Shabbat is not only about ensuring Jewish continuity in a survivalist sense; it is also about keeping Jews on our singular moral mission: the mandate to honor the inner dignity of all people.

So what does it mean to "keep" Shabbat today? The Socheshever Rebbe, the son-in-law of the Kotzker Rebbe, once remarked, "You can keep every [Shabbat] to the letter of the law, but unless [Shabbat] reaches the deepest and highest place in your heart, you haven't kept [Shabbat]."[22] Indeed, one dimension of keeping Shabbat today is internalizing the dignity of all laborers in our workplaces and in our homes.

NOTES

1 *Mishnah, Sanhedrin* 4:22.
2 *Babylonian Talmud, Bava M'tzia* 112a.
3 Rabbeinu Yonah, *Sefer HaYirah.*
4 *Babylonian Talmud, Bava Kama* 116b.
5 *Babylonian Talmud, Bava M'tzia* 83a.
6 Abraham Joshua Heschel, *The Sabbath: Its Meaning for Modern Man* (New York: Farrar, Strauss and Giroux, 1977), 13, 28.
7 Erich Fromm, *You Shall Be as Gods: A Radical Interpretation of the Old Testament and Its Tradition* (New York: Henry Holt, 1991).
8 Aryeh Kaplan, *Sabbath: Day of Eternity* (New York: National Conference of Synagogue Youth, 1974).
9 *Mishnah, Pirkei Avot* 1:10.
10 *Avot D'Rabbi Natan* 11.
11 *Avot D'Rabbi Natan* 11.
12 Joseph B. Soloveitchik, *Halakhic Man*, trans. Lawrence Kaplan (Philadelphia: Jewish Publication Society, 1983), 101.
13 For more, see Seth Masket, "How Leisure Time Transformed Society and Politics," *Pacific Standard*, October 2, 2017, https://psmag.com/economics/how-leisure-time-transformed-society-and-politics.
14 Dean Schabner, "Americans: Overworked, Overstressed," *ABC News*, May 2000, accessed April 17, 2018, http://abcnews.go.com/US/

story?id=93604&page=1#.T-JVJhxdWEt.

15 "The Land of Leisure; Work and Play," *Economist*, February 2, 2006, https://www.economist.com/node/5476124.

16 Steve Yoder, "Is America Overworked?," *Fiscal Times*, February 16, 2016, http://www.thefiscaltimes.com/Articles/2012/02/16/Is-America-Over-worked.

17 Baruch Epstein, *Makor Baruch*, part 4.

18 Maimondes, *Sh'monah P'rakim* (Introduction to *Pirkei Avot*), 5.

19 Rabbeinu Bachya, *Kad Kemach*, *Tamari*, 31.

20 Joseph B. Soloveitchik, "Majesty and Humility," *Tradition* 17, no. 2 (Spring 1978): 33–34.

21 ("רפ"ו ,העם אחד כותבי כל) ".אותם השבת שמרה השבת את שמרו משישראל יותר"

"Technology Shabbats"

Unplugging in a Hyper-Connected World

TIFFANY SHLAIN

I MAY BE the last person you'd expect to advocate for unplugging. I founded the Webby Awards, which has honored the best of the Web for the past twenty-two years, and served as the on-air Internet and technology expert for *Good Morning America* in the nascent days of the Web, explaining how this new technology was going to change everything in our lives. I advised then-Secretary of State Hillary Clinton about the Internet and technology. My film studio creates global days of film, discussion, and action, pushing the edge of new technologies to connect people around the world in innovative ways, so that they can have united conversations about the most important issues of our days. My husband, Ken Goldberg, is a robotics professor at UC Berkeley, and we live in the Bay Area, tech ground zero. We are often the first people to get a new technology and experiment with its uses. We are deeply immersed in everything having to do with technology.

It was actually Ken who introduced me to Shabbat as a weekly break from work when we met in 1997. I was shocked when he said, "I don't work on Saturdays; it's Shabbat. We need a day off." He had lived in Israel, and it made an impression on him that everything would shut down on Shabbat. During the week, he was an overworked grad student busy studying robotics at the Technion, but on Saturdays, with the buses gone and stores closed, he would paint, read, and relax. He loved it.

I was impressed to hear this from him. It struck me as profound, as well as sexy. Sexy to have deep wisdom guide him . . . and as a Jew who never practiced Shabbat growing up and who leaned to the agnostic side of things, I was intrigued. We fell in love, got married, and had our first child, Odessa. Let's just say we were focused on building ourselves and building a life together, and eventually the screens stayed on seven days a week. I remember that the day we went from our flip phones to iPhones, I struggled to convey to Ken why I felt like opening them would be a detriment to our relationship. But of course, we opened the Pandora's boxes, and soon, we were mainlining data, texts, e-mails, and calls like everyone else.

And like everyone else, we got addicted. We might compare the sense of technological dependency—the feeling that we must be accessible and responsive at any time—to that of drugs and alcohol. It's all because of the hormone dopamine, which is related to mood, attention, and desire (whether it's for knowledge, food, or sex). When you experience something and it feels good, dopamine tells you that you want more of it. When you're up late, clicking from website to website, or compulsively texting or e-mailing, it's reinforcing dopamine-induced loops. And as we have discovered the hard way, just as we can have too much sugar or too much alcohol, we can have too much information.

Thoughtful screen use is so important now, when people are more plugged in than ever. Almost four billion people—more than half the world's population—are connected to the Internet. For the most part, this is a good thing. We can easily stay connected with friends and family far away, we have unfettered access to all the ideas that came before us, and we can engage in real time with a global network of people and ideas, facilitating the cross-disciplinary thinking that is producing unprecedented advances. But there are downsides. Many are starting to worry about the effects of unlimited technology. According to recent studies from Nielsen and Deloitte, Americans are on their screens an average of over ten hours daily—around seventy-four hours a week—and check their phone forty-seven times a day (eighty-six times a day if they're under age twenty-four).[1] People are looking for help taming the techno-beast.

Unlimited screen time is bad for kids and adults alike. Almost every week, there's a new news report from a former Facebook, Google, or Twitter executive arguing that we have to impose some limits on the time we spend on screens, online, and on social media. There is an increasing amount of research pointing to the effects of this massive shift, much of it troubling. A recent study by Holly B. Shayka and Nicholas A. Christakis found "both liking others' content and clicking links significantly predicted a subsequent reduction in self-reported physical health, mental health, and life satisfaction."[2] While the intention of social media is to move humanity forward, to experience *more* connection and more widespread meaning and purpose, research shows the effect is often the opposite: loneliness, stress, and *dis*connection.

Smartphones have been around long enough now that there are generations who won't remember life without them. This raises a lot of questions. What are the long-term effects on our kids? What are the long-term effects on us? And more urgently: What should we do about it? Parents, especially, are becoming alarmed by research showing how detrimental unchecked screen time can be to children's mental health as well as educational, neurological, and social development. Having turned off all screens one day a week for nearly a decade, I know what a top-to-bottom change it can bring, especially where kids are concerned. Ours have been raised with "Tech Shabbats," and in many ways it has inoculated them to cope in a tech-oversaturated world. We believe that this will help them thrive. It is like we have given them a superpower tool to protect them and give them strength for the rest of their lives.

"Thou Shalt Unplug"

Jews have contributed so many things to the world. Some are widely admired (like the Theory of Relativity, the polio vaccine, anthropology, and psychoanalysis), and others are more debatable (like Barbie dolls and gefilte fish). Our best contribution? For me, there is no question: it is Shabbat.

I know observant Jews have always kept a day of rest, but many of us (like the 41 percent of American Jews who identify as secular) tend to roll right by Shabbat. Yet our contemporary 24/7 society demands more from us: the risk of overstimulation and oversaturation require us to turn off the firehose of media, news, e-mails, tweets, posts, likes, texts, pings, notifications, and buzzes periodically so we can truly be protected by what Rabbi Abraham Heschel calls "a palace in time." We need to enter into that palace and shut the door for twenty-four hours.

That is exactly what my family has done for a decade. We call it "Technology Shabbat," a reinvented version of an ancient innovation. Turning off technology is a ritual that can give you back your attention and time and let you focus on what matters most: *the essence of Shabbat*.

In a way, Shabbat itself is a technology. Three thousand years ago, it was an invention that completely transformed the world. Before then, time had no pauses; it was day after day after day. The invention of Shabbat made it so each week ended with a day of rest. The run-on sentence of time got a period, and everyone got a chance to catch their breath and focus. Thousands of years later, Shabbat lets us be present with each other, appreciate the small things, daydream, find perspective, and think big-picture thoughts. Returning to a slower pace one day a week also lets us be more fully present on the other six.

I have great respect for wherever people fall on the spectrum from atheist to believer, but I strongly feel that whether you believe, do not believe, or are agnostic, it is advisable to consider ideas that have lasted millennia. The Ten Commandments are a perfect example, and it is worth noting that "remember the sabbath day and keep it holy" (Exodus 20:8) is number four. Four! That's pretty high up on a list of ten! For me, personally, keeping this day without technology has been the best practice I have ever incorporated into my life. I get why it is in the top five. The Internet came along a few thousand years after the commandments, and "Thou shalt unplug" is not exactly the wording of the law. But it is definitely the spirit! And observing the

fourth commandment in the updated way of Tech Shabbat can renew
our spirits every week.

Here is what our house is like every Friday evening as we prepare
to close the door on that nonstop world: The smells of rosemary, gar-
lic, onions, chicken, and freshly baked challah fill the house. All the
piles of papers and books and laptops that normally lay claim to the
kitchen table are put away, and the table is set with freshly cut flowers, candles, and a tablecloth. When the doorbell rings, everything
gets powered down. Our daughter Blooma (age eleven) shuts down
the iPad, and Odessa (age seventeen) turns off her laptop. I usually
do one last tweet at sunset, telling people I am shutting down and
that I will "see them on the other side." Then I turn my phone off.
It takes a little bit to adjust. Sometimes, at the beginning of Friday
night, I have a phantom-limb-like sensation when I try to reach for a
phone that is not there, to look something up or make a call. I keep
a piece of paper out on the kitchen counter with a big black Sharpie,
and for the first couple of hours, I jot down whatever combination of
to-dos or reminders that tumble from my head. Then I feel set free,
with a full day of space to think and be—without responding to all
the news, dings, pings, buzzes, and notifications. A protected twenty-four hours.

Guests arrive and we sit down before a sumptuous meal. We light
the candles, sing the blessings (off-key), break the homemade challah, and discuss the world and the week. "What was one thing you
learned this week or one thing that you want to let go of? One thing
you are grateful for or one thing you are looking forward to next
week?" We answer in a clockwise conversation around the table,
everyone getting enough space and attention, as we treat time like a
special guest in our home.

The sleep of Friday night is the deepest sleep I have all week. We
spend the next day together: journaling, hanging, being in nature,
cooking, doing art projects, enjoying each other's company, or just
being. Later, maybe a bike ride, a nap, a board game, a great book. It's
the best day of the week.

Establishing our weekly Tech Shabbat was the best decision we ever made as a family and as individuals. This practice has enabled us to compartmentalize stress and ultimately reduce it, feel more creative, present, and happy, and be more productive for the rest of the week. Tech Shabbat makes the best day of the week feel longer and the rest of the week feel better. It is like having a metaphysical remote control that lets you slow down the good parts and fast-forward through the commercials.

A lot of people are looking for something like this. They're flocking to yoga studios, meditation retreats, and tech detox camps, seeking environments that help them turn off their phones. People are craving this space to be present. There has also been a renaissance of old concepts made new for the modern age, everything from meditation to growing your own food. People are hungry for updated versions of the old ways—ways like our Shabbat. Even *Vogue* magazine agrees: "Shabbat . . . is for everyone. It is an ancient antidote to our modern ailments."[3]

The revolutionary act of unplugging one day every week is simple and transformative. As Anne Lamott says, "Almost everything will work again if you unplug it for a few minutes, even you."[4]

It took me a while to find my way here, however.

Over a decade ago, I needed a drastic change. Within days of each other, my father, Leonard Shlain, whom I was incredibly close to, died of brain cancer, and my husband's and my daughter, Blooma, was born. I was asked to articulate the colliding of these profound events in a six-word memoir: "Father's funeral. Daughter's birth. Flowers everywhere."

These life-altering events made me think about the brevity of our time here on this earth and question how I was spending it. I didn't like where we seemed to be headed, with everyone staring at screens instead of connecting with the people we love, sitting right in front of us. I needed a revolution to transform the situation, and I found it. For twenty-four hours, my family and I went screen-free for the first National Day of Unplugging. That day was initiated by a Jewish organization I am a part of called Reboot, which brings together filmmakers, artists, comedians, and culture makers in order to rethink old rituals in new ways. Participating in the first National Day of Unplugging made us feel so renewed and present that we decided to make it a weekly practice. In many ways, this practice is our way of honoring my father. It gives us the space to think about the meaning of life and time and to be present with the people we love. To me, my father embodied all of those things.

In the beginning, we were the only family of that original group from Reboot who kept it going each week, but by now we have company. The need for unplugging and interest in Tech Shabbat has only snowballed with each addictive app that rolls down from the techno hills of Silicon Valley right into our hands.

With nearly a decade of perspective, it is easy to see how the practice has changed me and our family. Our daughters have grown up with Tech Shabbat. They are not struggling with the issues that are plaguing so many of their peers. They do not scroll through conversations. They read for pleasure. They know how to make small talk and eye contact. And if you are picturing two girls with plastic cones around their necks, like dogs, trying to keep them from scratching the techno itch, be assured they are normal kids with friends and social lives. As for me, I feel more balanced, calmer. Turning my phone off does not feel like amputating a limb anymore.

Our day without technology is a day I now run toward each week. I rush to s l o w d o w n. I look forward to the quality of presence: the way time stretches out, the way we connect, the way we can put our minds in a different mode. We can read without distractions. We invite guests and ask that they do not pull out their phones. It is funny how often they want to show us something on the phone. But each time, they pause, say "no phones," we nod yes, and then they smile and figure out a way to share verbally. It is nice, simple, and old-school.

That is how it goes, every week, for the last ten years. As Dov Seidman writes, "When you press the pause button on a machine, it stops. But when you press the pause button on human beings, they start."

NOTES

1 *2017 Global Mobile Consumer Survey: US edition*, Deloitte, https://www2. deloitte.com/content/dam/Deloitte/us/Documents/technology-media-telecommunications/us-tmt-2017-global-mobile-consumer-survey-executive-summary.pdf.

2 H. B. Shakya and N. A. Christakis, "Association of Facebook Use with Compromised Well-Being: A Longitudinal Study," *American Journal of Epidemiology* 185, no. 3 (February 1, 2017): 203–11, https://www.ncbi.nlm.nih.gov/pubmed/28093386; Holly B. Shakya and Nicholas A. Christakis, "A New, More Rigorous Study Confirms: The More You Use Facebook, the Worse You Feel," *Harvard Business Review*, April 10, 2017, https://hbr.org/2017/04/a-new-more-rigorous-study-confirms-the-more-you-use-facebook-the-worse-you-feel.

3 Ariel Okin, "How to Host a Shabbat Dinner and Why You Should—Even if You Aren't Celebrating," *Vogue*, March 9, 2017, https://www.vogue.com/article/how-to-host-friday-shabbat-dinner.

4 Anne Lamott, "12 Truths I Learned from Life and Writing," TED2017, April 2017, https://www.ted.com/talks/anne_lamott_12_truths_i_learned_from_life_and_writing.

FIFTH COMMANDMENT

כַּבֵּד אֶת־אָבִיךָ וְאֶת־אִמֶּךָ לְמַעַן יַאֲרִכוּן
יָמֶיךָ עַל הָאֲדָמָה אֲשֶׁר־יהוה אֱלֹהֶיךָ
נֹתֵן לָךְ:

Honor your father and your mother, that you
may long endure on the land that the Eternal
your God is assigning to you.

—Exodus 20:12

Honoring Your Father and Mother

Rabbi Laura Geller

I HAVE A DISTINCT and surprising memory from childhood of asking my father why the Ten Commandments says that the reward for honoring your parents is a longer life. It is surprising because my father was not a particularly religious man, and I didn't often ask him questions like that. What made it distinct was his answer. He told me, "Honoring your parents is harder than it sounds. Even though I love my mom and dad, your Nana Stella and Papa Sam, it isn't always easy to honor them, to take care of them, and to do some of the things they want me to do when I am also taking care of you and Mom. But I bet that because you and your brothers see Mom and me taking care of our parents now that they are old, you will take care of us when we get old . . . and so we will live longer."

He was right. Before my father died in his early eighties, my brothers and I did take care of him as he aged. We are still taking care of my ninety-six-year-old mother. And he was right that taking care of parents and figuring out what it means to honor them is actually harder than it seems.

Our tradition, as well as my father, understood how complicated honoring parents could be. The commandment appears three times in Torah: in the two different versions of the Ten Commandments (Exodus 20:12 and Deuteronomy 5:16), as well as a third time in Leviticus 19:3. In Exodus and Deuteronomy it says, "Honor your father and your mother," whereas in Leviticus, it says, "You shall each revere your mother and your father . . . I the Eternal am your

God." The Talmud asks, "Why add 'I the Eternal am your God'?" The answer: "There are three partners in creating a human being: the Holy One, the father, and the mother. The Holy One says, 'When a person honors one's father and one's mother, it is as though they are honoring Me.'"[1]

No wonder it sometimes feels as though we need to be angels to really honor our parents: the standard seems to be superhuman.

According to these Rabbinic ancestors, there is a significant difference between "honor" and "revere." "Revere" relates to maintaining a parent's dignity, while "honor" means caring for a parent's physical needs—food, clothing, and safety. But then the Rabbis ask, "At whose expense do you care for parents' physical needs, and at whose expense do you maintain parents' dignity?" Their answer: we care for parents' physical needs out of our parents' savings, at least until they run out of money, and we maintain our parents' dignity at our own expense, through the gift of our time and presence.

Of course, most of us want to make sure that our parents' physical needs are taken care of and that they maintain their dignity. But how do we translate these values into real-life experience, especially given all the other demands on our time and attention? How is it different if we live far away? What if it gets in the way of caring for our own children or grandchildren? What happens if our siblings or our own partners disagree on how it should be done? What are the particular challenges if our relationship with our parents is difficult, strained, or estranged?

What Is Enough?

Honoring and revering our aging parents can be overwhelming, and we may be inclined to ask ourselves: how much is enough? Our Rabbinic ancestors recognized the problem but couldn't agree on the answer. One rabbi said there are no lengths too great, and another acknowledged that some demands from our parents are simply irrational or impossible to fulfill. So it is up to us to set our limits based on our resources—financial, geographical, emotional—and those of our parents and siblings. For the needs that extend beyond what we can handle, we must find other ways to provide that care.

This is not just a modern problem. Maimonides (the twelfth-century Jewish sage) specifically ruled that a child can pay others to look after a parent if it is too distressing for the child to do so on his or her own.[2] Perhaps knowing that this has been a problem for adult children and their parents for so many generations can ease our own feelings of guilt and distress that we may not be able to provide the hands-on care our parents might want and need from us. But even so, not all of us have the financial resources to hire caregivers and care managers.

Because there are few government resources available to families with aging parents, most families simply cobble together a care-giving plan as best they can. If adult children (and their spouses) are willing to share the responsibility of caregiving, the financial and emotional burden on the adult children might be eased a bit. If not, one adult child generally ends up shouldering the entire financial and emotional burden, including interviewing and choosing prospective caregivers, introducing them to aging parents, and working them into the family routine. Many adult children also find that they must do all the shopping for their aging parents, maintain their parents' house (if the parents insist on remaining in their own home), take care of bill paying, and handle or oversee every other detail of their parents' lives. Most caregivers end up spending thousands of dollars of their own money in this effort, either through direct outlays, lost wages, or having to give up jobs or businesses entirely.

So besides saving for children's college tuition and your own retirement, it might also make sense to set aside money to help cover the cost of care for aging parents. Caregiving—especially round-the-clock, in-home care—is very pricey, and few elderly people have saved enough to cover that cost themselves. If you don't need to dip into that savings account, so much the better.

Whatever our financial resources, there is also the real challenge of our emotional resources—how much time, energy, and even physical strength we have in order to both honor and revere our parents. How do we deal with our own guilt or the sadness in our parent's voice when she says, "I wish you didn't have to go home so soon"?

After my father died, my mother's first instinct was to stay in the home they had shared. Honoring her desire to be independent and at the same time worrying about her safety living alone was a delicate dance for me and my brothers. But when she went out for an errand and left the kettle on, she understood that she couldn't live alone anymore. In a way, we were lucky that happened; she came to the conclusion on her own. Our friends have had a harder time convincing their aging parents that it was time to move.

My mother, now ninety-six, lives in a retirement community, and my brothers and I are continually trying to figure out the best ways to work as a team. One of us has taken over her finances and coordinates her health care. We have a skilled patient advocate to manage her doctor appointments and supervise her caregivers, who enable her to stay in the independent living section, because she refuses to move to assisted care. My brothers and I consult regularly via phone with each other and with the patient advocate, the social worker in her community, and, most recently, the hospice nurse and my mother's primary caregiver. My brother and I, who live far away, call my mother every day and visit as often as we can. Still, it feels as though I am never doing enough. And still, sometimes, my brothers and I disagree on what's best for her.

As we deal with the challenges of our parents' aging, we need to take a breath and allow ourselves to be present in the moment, paying attention not only to what is happening with our parents but also with ourselves and our siblings. We need to recognize our own sadness as we see our parents, who might have once been so vibrant in our minds and lives, becoming frail and dependent. It's also necessary, scary as it may be, to accept and face our fears about our own aging and mortality that our parents' situations raise for us. With self-awareness, these experiences can help us grow in wisdom and understanding.

Some Steps for Making Decisions about Our Parents

At least 25 percent of adult children are involved with the care of a parent, and the care we provide often changes as our parents—and we—age. When we were younger we were called the "sandwich generation," sandwiched between our young children, our work, and our parents. Now, as we are pressed harder—between frail parents needing our attention, adult children often looking for our help, and dealing with our own health issues and those of our partners and friends—the sandwich has become a panini.

In *Facing the Finish: A Road Map for Aging Parents and Adult Children*, life transitions expert Sheri Samotin outlines some steps that can help us as we care for our aging parents.

STEP 1: Assessment

Ask yourself some of these questions:

- Is my focus on both parents or just one? If both are still alive and still together, do I expect one to care for the other? If a move to a higher level of care is necessary for one, what are the implications for the other?
- What are my parents' physical, cognitive, and emotional conditions?
- What financial and human resources are available to provide help?
- Should I consider asking my parents to move closer to me, or should I consider moving closer to them?
- Do I understand that my parents, as long as they are cognitively capable, are entitled to make their own decisions, even if they make "bad" ones, and that I don't get to take over?

STEP 2: Clarity

Get clear about what you are willing and able to do for your parents, given the other demands on you. Obviously, if you are partnered, have siblings, or are the parent of adult children, decisions such as these need to be shared with your partner and siblings and perhaps your own children, since these will affect them too. It's even more challenging with blended families.

STEP 3: Conversation

Talk with your siblings and other loved ones who are closely involved with such decisions. These conversations are complicated, and it's easy to fall back into old patterns that might have been beneficial when you were children but are less useful now. Whatever you can do to get on the same page is worth doing, including talking with friends who have navigated similar situations, with a professional counselor, or with trusted clergy to help you avoid stepping on what might be old land mines, such as how you felt you were treated as a child or whom Mom or Dad really does love best.

Then you can move on to the more practical questions, such as what skills and availability you each have that could be useful to your parents. If the time comes when your parents need direct help, which of you ought to be doing what? Who ought to be paying bills, managing their financial affairs, interacting with doctors and others involved with your parents' lives? Do you imagine that your partners or children will also have some responsibility for your parents? What are your parents' financial resources, and what are your and your siblings' expectations of how they ought to be used? Should you consult with a professional who can lay out for you and your siblings the options that might be available to your parents?

STEP 4: More Conversation

As you (and your siblings and other loved ones) become clearer about the next steps for your aging parents, and ideally before a crisis occurs, begin discussing care plans with your parents. Samotin sets out some best practices for these ongoing conversations, including choosing the right time (for example, not in the midst of a family celebration) and deciding in advance who will facilitate (for example, you, your sibling, or an objective facilitator). Most important at this stage is to try to imagine what this transition is like for your parents, who might deny that they need any special help or need to make changes in their lifestyle. This is not a one-time conversation but an ongoing discussion.

A few years after my mother had been living in her new home but was still driving, we had another conversation. It was obvious to everyone, except my mother, that she shouldn't be driving anymore. My brothers and I decided to encourage her to give her car to her granddaughter as a graduation gift. At first our mother protested: How would she get around? How could she still be independent?

We shared with her research we had done about ride-sharing options in the community where she lived, and we showed her how to access gogograndparents.com, which makes it easy for a person who doesn't have a smartphone to use any phone to call an Uber or Lyft. Over time, and especially after her granddaughter made an impassioned request, she relented, eventually feeling very generous as opposed to incompetent and—this was key—able to explain to her friends why she was giving up her car in a way that made her feel good. It was certainly a more elegant solution than just taking away her keys.

Remembering and Appreciating

Now, some nine years after gifting her car to my daughter, my mother, safe in her graduated care retirement community, has Alzheimer's disease.

My mother is becoming more childlike as she ages, and she seems to enjoy singing songs she remembers from when she was younger. On a recent visit I reminded her of a song my dad used to sing to her:

> Believe me if all those endearing young charms
> which I gaze on so fondly today
> were to change by tomorrow and flee from my arms
> like fairy gifts fading away.
> Thou would still be adored
> as this moment thou art
> let thy loveliness fade as it will
> and around the dear ruins each wish of my heart
> would entwine itself verdantly still. (Lyrics by Thomas Moore)

In the middle of singing it with her, I burst into tears, gazing as I was on her fading self, these "dear ruins," remembering my late father, and, yes, imagining a time in the future when one of my children will be singing those words to me. Then my mother asked me what "verdantly" meant. I told her it meant she was still growing, and that made her smile.

Her adult children are still growing, too.

"Honor your father and your mother, that you may long endure on the land that the Eternal your God is assigning to you" (Exodus 20:12). The Torah doesn't tell us that it is easy or that all the solutions will be elegant. But it does suggest that there is a reward. For me the reward is not that I will necessarily have a longer life, but that I will have a more peaceful heart.

NOTES
1   *Babylonian Talmud, Nidah* 31a.
2   Maimonides, *Mishneh Torah, Hilchot Mamrim* 6:10.

Navigating the New Life Stage of Caregiver

Rabbi Richard F. Address

RIGHT NOW, in living rooms, kitchens, and rabbi's offices, families are gathering to deal with one of the challenges of modern life: longevity. The phenomenon of longevity has resulted in a new life stage, one that can last, more often than not, for years: serving as caregiver for parents or even multiple generations of family. The personal, spiritual, and financial impact of this life stage is a systemic issue for many families. The commandment to "honor" and "respect" our parents carries over to those who must care for a spouse, friend, relative, or child. The values of dignity and sanctity, so basic to our understanding of interpersonal relationships, can often become blurred and gray in specific cases. Furthermore, behind the stress of caregiving lurks the often not-too-repressed fear of "Will this be me someday? And if so, who will care for me?"

A November 2017 AARP study indicated that "four in ten caregivers say that they were not prepared to take on the role of family caregiver. Among those who were prepared, only 16% say they were very prepared."[1] Likewise, the same study showed that caregivers experienced a wide range of emotions. "Positive emotions such as being pleased they are able to help (91%) far outweighed the negative. However, over half are stressed (51%) or worried (51%) and many are overwhelmed (40%)."[2]

The stresses and strains of caregiving on the caregiver and the family often manifest themselves suddenly. In an instant, a family's world can be changed and roles reimagined. Not surprisingly, "when asked if they had a choice in taking on their caregiving role, half of the respondents said no."[3] Caregiving can also have distinct economic implications for families and individuals. The cumulative cost of time taken off from work, home health aides, alternative living arrangements, and other associated expenses underscores the fact that most of us are only one medical or caregiving crisis away from serious financial concerns.

Another study, this one by the AARP Public Policy Institute and the National Alliance for Caregiving, also reflected the reality of this caregiving crisis.[4] The study showed that some forty million Americans provide unpaid care to an adult and that about 10 percent of caregivers are themselves over seventy-five. While the typical caregiver is a woman about fifty years of age, some 40 percent of current caregivers are men, and an increasing number of caregivers are people between eighteen and thirty-four. The multigenerational nature of caregiving has led our program, Jewish Sacred Aging, to refer to this reality not as the "sandwich generation," but as the "club sandwich generation." It is no longer unusual for a person in their sixties to be caring for a parent in their eighties or nineties, while simultaneously helping their adult children, perhaps also their grandchildren, and managing their own life on top of all of this.

The calm and insightfulness of our own tradition counterbalance these challenges. The commandment to "honor" (*kabeid*; Exodus 20:12; and Deuteronomy 5:16) and "revere" or "respect" (*tira-u*; Leviticus 19:3) our parents is repeated three times in Torah and forms the basis for an approach to the challenges of the caregiver life stage. Underlying the texts, the discussions, and the commentaries is a fundamental ethic that I suggest is the foundation for all of our current discussions that look at aspects of personal and medical ethics: the dignity and sanctity of human life and its preservation in dignity and sanctity. This fundamental ethic leads us to the basic belief that we must do everything we can to ensure the dignity of another person, who, created *b'tzelem Elohim* ("in the image of God"), deserves that honor and respect. In practice, however, many of us face the challenge of honoring and respecting that idea and ideal of dignity when the circumstances threaten to overwhelm us.

The Torah's injunctions are expanded in a series of discussions in the Talmud. In the Babylonian Talmud, *Kiddushin* 31b–32a formulates an interesting and powerful approach to unpacking the Torah's dual commandments to honor and respect one's parents. Respect is understood to mean not sitting or standing in a parent's usual place and not contradicting them in the midst of a dispute. Honor, in the Talmudic discussion, means that the adult child is obligated to provide a parent with food, drink, and clothing, as well as assistance in going and coming from their home. Again, the idea of ensuring a person's dignity is fundamental to these conclusions. The subjective nature of this Talmudic discussion is played out every day in families as one's standard of dignity can (and often does) change as a person ages and as the circumstances of their care and needs evolve.

We often speak of "quality of life" in the context of dignity. Yet, we know people whose definition of their own "quality" changes over time. Indeed, one of the current debates and challenges in dealing with dementia and Alzheimer's goes directly to this issue. It is, at the heart of the subject, a spiritual one. How often have we heard a caregiver of a person dealing with end-stage Alzheimer's lament that this is "no way to live" and that their loved one has "no more quality of life"? How we honor the words of the commandment will say much about relationships and wishes. Making choices that dignify and sanctify life are often choices between bad and worse. Yet, this reality also underscores the importance of seeing each case within the context of a person's life and wishes.

This is another argument for families to do their best to have early conversations about caregiving and end-of-life wishes. Those conversations should include a discussion of how and by whom the care of loved ones is to be shouldered. Who will do what and when, given that one's geographical proximity to a person needing care does not necessarily mean that individual is the one to be the designated caregiver? That role often is assigned to a person in a family who had that role, in some way, as they grew up. Add to all of this the challenges of caregiving long-distance or as an only child, and you can begin to imagine some of the challenges that so many families now have to navigate.

The Talmudic discussion in *Kiddushin* anticipates many of the issues that modern caregivers face. In the discussion the Talmud asks, "Who pays?" The Rabbis conclude that if an adult parent has the ability to help pay for the costs of their care, then they are obliged to do so. "For a child to say to a greatly diminished parent 'I'll pay' when the parent still has his personal assets is murderous. It kills the parental self. Here is the last framework in which the parent can be a self-directing, self-supporting person, and the child refuses to allow him or her that right and pleasure. . . . If the mitzvah to revere one's parents means anything, then the parent pays if he or she can."[5] How then, does the adult child "pay"? We pay through the giving of time, such as taking time off from work, to accompany a loved one to an appointment or treatment. The amount of time spent in family caregiving translated into economic impact is staggering. The National Alliance for Caregiving calculated that in 2009, the value of the services provided by family caregivers was $375 billion a year.[6]

In the caregiving revolution we also confront issues of conflict between what a parent may wish for themselves and what their adult child(ren) may wish for them. Again, the need for conversation before these issues arise is paramount. Tradition, too, offers guidance in resolving these conflicts, under the concept of the *shomeir*, a word that has the meaning, in this context, of "caregiver, guardian." We are mandated to honor and respect the wishes of our adult parents. These wishes, made by competent adults and reflective of their understanding of dignity, must be honored. For example, if a parent has prepared documentation that states his or her wishes for future care and has done so while cognizant of the choices being made, "the failure to implement these instructions is a violation of reverent obedience."[7]

We are commanded to honor and respect our parents. We are not, however, commanded to love them. Can we acquire any guidance from tradition for when we are faced with an aging parent who may need our help, but who acted in ways that contradicted basic values and fabric of decency? The commandment to "honor" and "respect" becomes less obligatory in these difficult and emotionally fraught cases, when weighed against the understanding that the adult child is also created *b'tzelem Elohim* and has the right to make decisions such that they will not be crushed under the weight of undue obligation. This very real scenario is confronted by clergy regularly. Dr. Michael Chernick of Hebrew Union College–Jewish Institute of Religion offers this interpretation:

> Indeed, the commandments of respect and honor are incumbent upon children only when parents observe the commandments required of them. An attack upon the source of Jewish values, the Torah, by the parent invalidates the parent's rights provided by that source. Parents who have been irresponsible, cruel, neglectful, and harmful to their children have failed to uphold their obligations in Jewish law and practice to their children. Hence, they have forfeited the "honor" and "respect" with which Jewish law entitles them.[8]

Often, during family discussion about future living arrangements, downsizing, and care, a parent will turn to their adult child(ren) and admonish them, "I trust you to do the right thing, but don't you ever put me in one of those places" (by which they mean a home for the elderly); yet, so many of us reach a point when it becomes impossible, for a variety of reasons, to maintain the role of primary caregiver. Logistics, finances, changes in family dynamics, and the caregiver's own aging, along with the increasing frailty of the loved one, can contribute to making the task of living the commandment difficult, if not impossible. "If Dad falls, can I pick him up the right way?" "As Mom's dementia worsens, can I guarantee her safety?" So many families have made promises to a loved one, but when circumstances change, the prospect of ceding care to a third party may become a necessity. The twelfth-century commentator, philosopher, and physician Maimonides actually gives guidance for this particular dilemma that still resonates for so many families today:

> One whose father or mother has become mentally impaired should try to treat them according to their mental ability with pity for them. But if he cannot stand it, because they have

become too deranged, he should leave them and go, directing
others to treat them appropriately.[9]

Applied to our times, one can see within Maimonides's statement
the permission, within certain contexts, to cede care to professionals, facilities, or others when we can no longer ensure care that
maintains the dignity and safety of a loved one. These are rarely easy
decisions, but we can look to a hierarchy of values as a guide. Our
fundamental responsibility is to preserve the dignity and sanctity of
human beings, and sometimes that end is best served by entrusting
a loved one to a facility. Increasingly, there are resources available to
help clergy as they seek to aid a congregant. AARP has a wealth of
information, as do local Jewish Family and Children's Services. Likewise, Area Agencies on Aging can be a valuable resource.

These difficult decisions and challenging life situations often surprise us by opening a window to meaningful spiritual encounters.
There are moments when adult children become aware that the
roles to which they have been accustomed may be changing. They are
charged with the awareness that they are being given the opportunity
to care for the people who cared for them. This transitional moment
can be transformational as well. Past hurts or estrangements are
sometimes resolved as the reality of mortality becomes clear and
time takes on new meaning.

As caregiving challenges and concerns arise, it seems that there
is a growing awareness of a need to have this life stage acknowledged within a spiritual context. Accordingly, we are witnessing an
increased interest in prayers and rituals associated with caregiving.
To that end, here is a prayer that speaks to the concerns, hopes, and
fears that swirl within each context of caring for someone:

> Sustainer of the Universe, help me to care for my loved one
> with hope, courage and sensitivity.
> Grant me insight, resourcefulness and the ability to ask for
> help and to accept help when it is needed.
> May I find the patience to overcome difficult moments
> and to find meaning and purpose in the smallest task.

O Eternal God
help me to remember to take care of myself so that I
may take care of others.
Be with me and my loved one
as we journey on this path together.
May the One who makes peace in the heavens,
bring peace to me, to my family and loved ones,
and to us all.[10]

As baby boomers age and the caregiving challenges mount, congregations will be called upon to be even more present in the life of our people. The power of faith communities to support individuals and families will be a major aspect of how we continue to evolve into sacred caring communities.

Notes

1   Laura Skufca, "AARP Family Caregiving Survey: Caregivers' Reflections on Changing Roles," AARP Research, November 2017, https://doi.org/10.26419/res.00175.001.
2   Ibid., Skufca, "AARP Family Caregiving Survey."
3   Emily Gurnom, "Who America's Caregivers Are and Why It Matters," Next Avenue, June 4, 2015, https://www.nextavenue.org/who-americas-caregivers-are-and-why-it-matters/.
4   *Caregiving in the U.S. 2015*, National Alliance for Caregiving and AARP Public Policy Institute, June 2015, https://www.aarp.org/content/dam/aarp/ppi/2015/caregiving-in-the-united-states-2015-report-revised.pdf.
5   Michael Chernick, "Who Pays? The Talmudic Approach to Filial Responsibility," in *That You May Live Long: Caring for Our Aging Parents, Caring for Ourselves*, ed. Richard F. Address and Hara E. Person (New York: URJ Press, 2003), 98.
6   *Caregiving in the U.S. 2015.*
7   Benjamin Freedman, *Duty and Healing: Foundations of a Jewish Bioethic* (New York: Routledge, 1999), 122. Freedman discusses the concept of the *shomeir* within Jewish tradition and the relationship of that concept to the role of caregiver (see pp. 175–76, 179–81).
8   Chernick, "Who Pays?," 101.
9   Maimonides, *Mishneh Torah, Hilchot Mamrim* 6:10.
10 Michele Brand Medwin, *Alzheimer's Families: Emotional and Spiritual Tools for Coping* (Binghamton, NY: Colchester Woods Press, 2018), 211.

Number Five

RABBI ANNIE BELFORD

I HAVE A FRIEND, an older and wiser colleague in town, who told
me that when her teenage children would talk back to her, she would
hold up her hand, fingers splayed, and shout, "Number five!" She
was reminding her children, in a way perhaps only rabbis would do,
that in talking back or refusing to listen or doing any of the myriad
small rebellions children engage in, they were breaking the fifth
commandment by not respecting their mother and father. I laughed
when she told me this, since my children were just toddlers at the
time, and their methods of disrespect came in the form of pacifiers
thrown to the floor or tantrums that passed in moments. The hands
I held up to them were for them to hold as we crossed a street, or
when their father and I counted, "One-two-three WOOOO!" before
swinging them gleefully in the air. The hands for respecting one's
parents, I thought, were the hands with which I gave my children
bubble baths or heated frozen pizzas (I am a working mom after all!);
they were the hands with which I rubbed their backs just as my mom
had rubbed mine when I was a child; they were the hands with which
I took tender care of my child. I had years, I thought, until I would
raise my own hand, fingers splayed, and shout, "Number five!" to my
own teens.

My own ideas of how my hand—"Number five!"—related to honoring parents changed radically on December 13, 2017, when I held
my own mother's hand in the emergency room. I had received a text
from her around 8:30 a.m., after dropping my now elementary-aged
kids off at school and seeing my oldest off to middle school. "I'm on
the floor!" my mom texted. "Is this a joke?" I wrote back. "No! I fell

at 2 a.m. and I can't get up!" A rushed drive to my mom's house led to a 911 call, which led to an ambulance ride to the ER and a flurry of scans. After hours passed, the ER doctor returned with a neurologist. I had been with enough families in enough hospital rooms to know that this was not a good sign. Heaviness descended on me, and clarity too. "There is a mass in your brain, and it is pressing on the part of your brain that controls your motor function. That's why you can't move your legs. The radiologist thinks it might be glioblastoma, but we won't know until we do a biopsy." I held my mom's hand as the doctors spoke, and we made arrangements to get her admitted into the hospital and scheduled her biopsy. We waited a week for the results, but they only confirmed what I knew the moment those doctors walked into the room, the moment that feeling of heaviness and clarity descended: my mom had glioblastoma multiforme IV, and she was going to die.

The details of her cancer are perhaps not important, though they are becoming increasingly well known. John McCain had the same type of cancer, as did Beau Biden and Ted Kennedy. My father's best friend would be diagnosed with it just a few months after my mom. A beloved congregant had been nursed through it just a few years before. I knew, before speaking with any doctors, that this brain cancer was pernicious, aggressive, incurable, and difficult to treat. My mom's cancer seemed more so because her tumor could not be surgically removed. Instead, when the biopsy confirmed glioblastoma, we made plans for aggressive radiation and chemotherapy, kept our fingers crossed for alternative therapies, and arranged for her to move from her two-story condo into my first-floor bedroom. Driving home from the hospital after the biopsy, my mother said, "I just want to live to see Lev's bar mitzvah." That was nearly two years away, and I knew, no matter her course of treatment, she wouldn't make it that long. So I took her hand in mine again and said, "Mom, that's a really great goal. But I think our goal should just be to treasure every day we have together and do something you love every day. How does that sound?" She took a deep breath. She paused a moment. "It sounds good, Annie."

So that is exactly what we did. My mom could no longer live on her own, much less manage to walk up a flight of stairs to her bedroom, so she moved in with me and my children. She shared my bedroom in my newly single life, and at night, after I tucked in my kids, I would tuck in my mom. Or perhaps we tucked each other in; I made sure she had everything she needed within arm's reach, and then, as I got into bed, I would tell her about my day, unburden myself of all my stresses, talk through all of my uncertainties, and would often grab her hand across the bed and tell her how much I loved her. Nothing in my life seemed real until I told my mom, and in those months when she lived with me, everything seemed to come into hyper reality.

Everything *seemed* to mean more, because everything *did* mean more. In the mornings, I would help my mother shower, supporting her so she would not slip, toweling her dry because she could not bend over any longer. Growing up, my mother was beyond modest; she would not even change her clothes in front of me. Out of necessity all modesty was gone now, but without embarrassment. My mom shivered when she got out of the shower, so we bought a towel warmer, and I ran the shower as hot as it would go to get the bathroom as hot and steamy as a sauna. She still shivered when she emerged, and I helped her get dressed and fastened her bra, then made sure she would not slip as she shuffled with her walker to the toilet. When I dried her gray hair, together we would lament the clumps of hair that fell out and blew into the air with the blow dryer's hot blast, a devastating yet all-too-common side effect from the radiation. Then, in the evenings, I would help my six-year-old bathe, towel her lithe little body dry, and brush her long blonde hair, thick with youth and bouncy with health. The poignant contrasts between these daily rituals—just two among many—were not lost on me, and only served to heighten my ability to appreciate the moments I had with mother and my children.

The moments when my children barreled home from school each afternoon, with a chorus of "Hi, Nonnie!" and kisses on my mother's cheek, and her simple pleasure to be surrounded by their presence. The moments when my mom, a decades-long vegetarian, tucked into brisket and ribs and good ole Texas barbeque with gusto, prompting me and my children (decades-long vegetarians ourselves!) to smile and nod to my mother as we served more meat and (behind my mother's back) made gagging faces to each other. The moments when I whipped up platters of my now-famous brownies, with marshmallows and chocolate chips mixed in the batter, for my chocoholic mother and children to enjoy while I gamely passed them over, since I have never liked chocolate myself. The moments when we gathered around the TV to watch *The Goldbergs* or *Perfect Strangers* or *The Golden Girls* (as the tumor grew larger, my mom's sophisticated taste grew simpler and simpler, and the sitcoms of my childhood became her favorite things to watch). These moments of blessing were plentiful, and I prayed they would never end.

But of course, they did. There came the morning in April when my mom tried to get out of bed to go to the bathroom, and her legs failed her again. She slipped to the floor and could not stand up. She again had to be rushed to the ER, and we spent another week in the hospital. The tumor had grown, despite the aggressive treatments. The tumor was again pressing on the motor center of her brain, robbing her of all control of her legs. When the oncologist, my mom, and I spoke about hospice, her doctor left the room in tears. I just kept holding mom's hand.

I held my mom's hand as we celebrated Mother's Day in hospice, a day we had always spent together in the years since she moved to Houston. She always bought me a little gift, and I always bought her something, too. This year, it seemed pointless to buy her a gift; when would she even use it? Instead, I brought my children to visit, with our traditional Mother's Day brunch meal in hand: pancakes and her new favorite food of all time, bacon (believe me, the irony of the vegetarian rabbi's mother craving bacon was not lost on me!). I kept saying to myself, though, that honoring one's mother is one of the Ten Commandments, and not eating pork is much lower on the so-called list! Yes, it was a paltry justification. Did I feel guilty as I cut up the thick-cut bacon and fed it to my mama, who ate it with gusto, eating being the only motor skill she still had? Absolutely not. It was an honor to give her what she wanted; it was an honor to make her as happy as I could. So that Mother's Day, as we watched Disney movies on the TV in her room, I held her hand. I took a picture of her hand in mine and posted it on Facebook, writing, "There is nowhere else I would rather be."

It is interesting, as I look back, how much I long for that moment now. How much I long for every hand hold: The first time we drove to radiation, when my mom was so nervous (and so was I), and I just took her hand in mine and paid such close attention to how it felt. The skin of her hands, aged over sixty-nine years, wrinkled and crepe-y (her words, not mine!), and so soft from the daily moisturizer she rubbed into them. The way her fingers on my palm tapped the beat of the inane pop song playing on the radio until she calmed and simply held my hand in hers. The way I could feel her bones under her skin, even though she was not a thin woman, because her hands were always so delicate and small. I remember her hand in mine on that morning drive and on the morning of Mother's Day. I remember her hand reaching up to mine as I fed her queso from Torchy's Tacos, her favorite food in the last days of her life and the only thing she would eat. She could not hold the spoon, but she tried to hold my hand. I remember her hand holding mine when we had our last conversation, when she really could not speak anymore and rarely exited the fog into which her mind had descended, but when—for a brief moment—she was alert and aware. "Mom, remind me if you ever get a brain tumor again that we should move to Oregon!" She nodded vigorously; I think she hated lying powerless in that hospice bed more than I hated watching her lie powerless in that bed. I then told her about a difficult interaction I had had and asked her whether I had made the right choice—about that interaction, about my life choices—I think in that moment I was asking her approval about everything I had ever done. Again, she nodded vigorously, and that gave me deep reassurance. Then, as a wave of doubt entered my mind, I asked her, "Mom, do you know who I am?" She looked at me like I had grown another head and said, with just a bit of a struggle, "Anne Elizabeth Belford." She named me that day, a week before she died, just as she named me at birth, giving me her own mother's name, her mother who had died from cancer just months before I was born. She named me; she saw me; she knew me; she loved me. Those were the last words she ever spoke. She died a week later; I held her hand as she drew her last breath.

"Number five!" my friend would say, splaying her fingers in the air, reminding her slightly rebellious teens to honor their mother. I hold my hand up now and think, "Number five. Honor your father and your mother." I hold my hand up now, and it seems so empty. I hold my hand up and feel a shadow of my mom's hand there, overlaying my own, as I grab my own children's hands and walk with them toward tomorrow.

Sixth Commandment

לֹא תִרְצָח

You shall not murder.
—Exodus 20:13

"You Shall Not Murder"

Rabbi Harold L. Robinson

ABOUT TWENTY-FIVE YEARS AGO I was visiting a World War II veteran in a sailors' old-age home. He was elderly and frail but alert and articulate. His daughter sat next to the bed on his left, and I, a Navy chaplain in uniform, stood at the foot of the bed conversing with both. At some point he became focused only on me. He began to describe in gruesome detail the sinking of his ship, the total darkness, the rapid listing of the decks, the struggle to climb ladders at impossible angles, the last anguished soul-searing screams of buddies below deck as the watertight doors were slammed shut, dooming them to drown, his plunge into oily water, the flames, the frantic swimming to escape, and the blessed rescue hours later.

After my visit, the daughter accompanied me down the hall. With copious tears and bewildered, she sobbed that she remembered Dad's return home from the war and knew his ship had been sunk. But no one—not her mother nor her siblings—had ever heard the story. Looking at me with confusion she asked, "Why did he tell you, a stranger?" I answered, "My Navy uniform assured him I would understand his story and really empathize with his passion. Telling me, he never had to explain either the circumstances or his actions, nor his sense of guilt and remorse."

This assignment seemed straightforward: write an analysis of "You shall not murder" (Exodus 20:13) as a rabbi with thirty-six years of service with the U.S. Navy and U.S. Marine Corps. I would reference applicable Jewish sources and Western moral philosophy on when wars are justified and what actions by combatants crossed a moral boundary and became murder. It was straightforward until I submitted my draft to my colleagues in the congregational rabbinate. Vocabulary and cultural references that are the common means of expression in the military were surprisingly opaque to my readers; the categories under discussion such as "just war," meaning when a war is justified, and "justice in war," meaning what is justified in the conduct of belligerents of war, when is it being conducted in a just or unjust manner, needed explanation. Even the term "warrior" (those who go to war; Hebrew, *lochem*), the self-accepted and proudly borne appellation of every member of our military, was deemed offensive or too blunt for my civilian readers.

Please then be patient with my parenthetical illumination of terminology in the text. I have struggled to use only everyday language but at times tried to share with the reader the more precise military and philosophical language.

In Western thought, the subject is called *jus in bello*, "justice in war," as distinct from *jus ad bellum*, "just war." The latter deals with the causes, goals, and context of war and asks if it was defensive, preemptive, aggressive, and so forth—that is, whether or not the causes for going to war were just. The former speaks to the conduct of war: which weapons were used, how noncombatants and prisoners were treated, and whether the war was fought according to "the rules" (commonly understood as the Geneva Conventions). This distinction is important but somewhat artificial, since it begs the question: Can the actions of warriors be just and ethical if the war itself is unjust? And if the cause is just, is it ethical to risk defeat by adhering to theoretical or perhaps aspirational "laws" of war, or is "all fair in love and war"?[1]

Usually these questions are the stuff of volumes, not articles, so I propose to discuss only the sixth commandment's applicability to the individual warrior, not to war at large. Let us first define the issues that make this difficult before seeking to resolve them.

In Jewish teaching and tradition, human life is sacred, and murder, the unlawful taking of life, is prohibited. When Cain kills Abel, God responds, "What have you done? Your brother's bloods cry out to Me from the earth!" (Genesis 4:10).[2] The Talmud takes the plural "bloods" to indicate Abel's blood and that of his would-be descendants, in order to teach that whosoever destroys a single life has destroyed the world entire, and whosoever saves a single life has preserved the world entire.[3] How many sermons have been preached around this lofty premise? Less frequently preached, however, is another dictum in the Talmud, "When someone comes to kill you, rise up early and kill him first," and by extension, the obligation of a bystander to prevent murder by taking the life of the potential murderer (if absolutely necessary), all based on the killing of a nighttime robber in Exodus 22:1–2.[4]

How many worlds, then, are destroyed by dropping a single bomb? And even if the bombing was an act of self-defense, how does it justify the death of civilians? Even if we take an uncomplicated view of our sources and state that self-defense is permitted when absolutely necessary to preserve a life, that hardly seems to justify the warrior inflicting vast carnage and accepting collateral damage to noncombatant civilians.

Part of the difficulty comes in defining "unlawful" within a Jewish halachic or ethical context, particularly when it comes to the Jewish definition of murder. In Jewish tradition, murder is distinct from other sorts of sanctioned homicide, such as self-defense and court-imposed capital punishment. It is also distinct from accidental homicide, which, though usually illegal, is not murder. Murder, we imagine, is strictly defined and limited by the legal codes and scriptural text. However, biblical and Talmudic references offer numerous difficulties for modern readers.

Three possible examples of problematic texts in Scripture are as follows:

1. Yael "heroically" kills the sleeping (and perhaps both drugged and unarmed) Sisera in Judges 4:21. Could he not have been captured rather than killed?
2. When Samson brings down the Philistine temple at Dagon, which was "filled with men and women," many of those were presumably noncombatants (Judges 16:27–30).

Would that qualify Samson as a suicide terrorist today? What would distinguish Samson's actions from a captured enemy who kills the captors, civilians, and themself with smuggled explosives?

3. Samuel commands Saul in the name of the Eternal to "smite Amalek utterly, destroy all that they have; do not spare them, but kill both man and woman, infant and suckling" (I Samuel 15:3). This assault was revenge for the Amalekites' aggression against the Israelites in the wilderness many generations earlier (I Samuel 15:2). How do we think about multigenerational guilt? Does that revenge slaughter of an entire community qualify as genocide?

Chazal, our Sages of blessed memory, the authors of Mishnah, Talmud, and Midrash, are a likely source for a Jewish definition of murder (after all, Talmud is the source of our halachah). Chazal went to great extremes to define capital murder out of existence in all practical terms. They built very high legal barriers that prevented courts from finding a verdict of murder, a capital offense. Thus we read in the Mishnah, "A Sanhedrin that puts a man to death . . . is called a murderous one . . . even once in seventy years. And Rabbis Tarfon and Akiva added, 'If we had been in the Sanhedrin, no death sentence would ever have been imposed.'"[5]

Additionally, Chazal required two independent eyewitnesses and credible proof that the assailant was clearly made aware, in advance, of both the act's illegality and the severity of punishment for the impending crime. Thus in Jewish law, an assailant who was found standing over a corpse holding a bloody dagger and heard screaming, "He deserved to die," in the presence of an uninvolved third-party eyewitness testifying, "I told him not to do it; it's murder and a capital crime," could not be convicted of murder for the lack of a second witness and a second clearly conveyed warning.[6] While I believe that the Rabbinic creation of these likely unenforceable requirements for conviction provides strong evidence for the Sages' rejection of scripturally mandated capital punishment, they do not help define murder, the underlying crime.

Are we moderns then indeed left to our own devices to define murder? Thank God we are mostly insulated from the realities of violent death and explicitly of armed conflict. For most of us, most of the time, murder—indeed, all violent death—is troubling, even shocking, but very rarely personally witnessed. Our experience is most often only at a distance and conveyed thirdhand through the media. Despite our country being awash in deadly weapons, the murder rate in the United States is the lowest it has been in decades (4.5 per 100,000 people in 2015, down from 9.8 in 1974). We imagine wars occur in far-off places (9/11 and the like are shocking as exceptions), and fewer than 1 percent of our fellow Americans ever don a uniform, never mind deploy to combat. This modern American distance from armed conflict is very much a recent blessing. During World War II, our nation of 140 million inhabitants fielded an armed force of 18 million. One in eight of all Americans—men, women, children, and elders—were in uniform. Many Americans also had firsthand experience of war as refugees from European conflicts, World War I, World War II, and the revolutions of Tsarist Russia and Franco's Spain.

If for us, North Americans, violent death—especially murder and war—is rare and shocking, it follows that any rules we propose will seem irrelevant in the warrior's reality. For the warrior, deadly conflict is a ubiquitous, spectral presence. From the first moment of service, members are trained to kill the enemy and to avoid, if possible, becoming a casualty—to kill or be killed. The recruit is taught to recount the heroism of warriors who perished saving comrades or died holding fire when death came at the hands of a pre-adolescent with a concealed explosive vest. If the warrior is in fact sent to the combat theater, deadly conflict and death are no longer hypothetical concepts, but a pervasive reality, a part and parcel of everyday life; evacuations of the wounded, memorial services for the fallen, and the inherently inhumane and dehumanizing experience of taking another's life become commonplace. Yet, we mortal beings are simply not capable of grasping the life-changing moral impact of killing another human—even the enemy, even when the choice is to kill or be killed. It is simply not possible to convey with mere words the profoundly debilitating effect on most normal people of killing another human being; yet this is what we ask from some of our nation's most altruistic and idealistic young adults who join the armed forces committed to make the world safe for the rest of us.

Now, one last category of perplexing quandaries: how are our modern rules of warfare, such as the Geneva Conventions, applied to the modern battlefield? Most of our conventions preserve (even fossilize) the code of gallantry and honor idealized in biblical accounts and in tales of chivalric knights. War, at least conceptually, was once waged between armies of warriors who were expected to understand and accept its risks. Two examples come to mind. In Judges 7:3, Gideon sends home all who were fearful and trembling, thus ensuring only those with the capacity and willingness to accept or cope with the risks would go to battle. A second example is outlined by Shakespeare. In his play *Henry V* (act 4, scene 3), he writes that at Agincourt, Henry V first sends away, with pay, those "who have no stomachs for this fight" and then appeals to the valor and camaraderie of the remainder, "we few, we happy few, we band of brothers; for he that shed his blood with me shall be my brother." In both cases the soldiers know what they are getting into and give themselves freely to the battle. The unwilling and the noncombatants are not included in the fray. At least theoretically, wars were fought between warriors. Civilian casualties might have been expected, but their suffering was incidental.

That was the theory, but in fact in siege warfare, the hunger, despair, and suffering of the civilian population are intended means to mass destruction. In Western nineteenth-century wars, civilians were often caught in the middle, and the proponents of "gallant and honorable" warfare understood the plight of these civilian victims as an unfortunate but unavoidable reality, merely coincidental collateral damage. Other examples abound; for example, there were wars against "the uncivilized barbarians" (famously Native Americans, but also Southeast Asians, sub-Saharan Africans, and many others), who were unprotected by Western European notions and the rules of gallantry.

By the end of the twentieth century, most nineteenth-century premises had simply ceased to apply. By World War II, total war was waged against entire populations. Factories, along with their workers, became legitimate military targets. Where once cannons (never mind battering rams) might require weeks of bombardments to reduce defensive battlements, by World War II an aerial bombardment could destroy an entire city in a few days. Moreover, with the advent of nuclear weapons, a single payload of a lone bomber destroyed an entire city. More recently, weapons have been developed that deliver death to the enemy with pinpoint lethality at virtually no risk to the one aiming and firing the weapon. During the first Gulf War, we witnessed—through broadcast news footage—cruise missiles penetrating target windows hundreds of miles from their launch sites. Today, drones flown by pilots from the comfort of U.S. suburban bases kill enemy warriors on distant continents, killing civilian leaders and, if need be, those who happen to be nearby.

New realities of war have forced conceptual changes. Wars—our wars—are often not between two or more nation-states; non-state actors are enormously empowered. In modern asymmetric warfare, civilians become combatants and engage regular troops in ways that seem antithetical to both our European conventions and our ability to understand the new reality. These conceptual challenges include guerilla warfare, suicide bombers, and child soldiers. Yet we recall with pride the American patriots at Lexington and Concord, armed civilians who picked off the British from behind rocks and trees. Were they not guerilla warriors? What is the modern warrior to do when charged by tens of thousands of civilians, some of whom are literally babes in their mothers' arms, mixed in with armed enemy combatants dressed in civilian garb? (Please remember we are discussing only the warrior's role, *jus in bello*; we are not discussing *jus ad bellum*, the legitimacy of the war that creates the warrior's circumstances.) How do they know the waving young child approaching their guard post is not equipped with a remote-controlled suicide vest? Parenthetically, there is no reality to the suggestion that the warrior aim for the feet of a charging mob. While in fact they may do just that, not even the most highly skilled marksman can "only wound" runners in a charging mob at hundreds of meters. Indeed, we are a long way from the fields of Agincourt, or Waterloo, or even Verdun.

Here is what I have learned from countless conversations with our warriors (our soldier sailors, airmen, Marines, and Coasties) and from my own very limited field experience. First, the warrior deserves rules—even rules that bring risk to the warrior and comrades—precisely because rules help warriors preserve their own humanity. The disconnects between basic human nature and the realities of battlefield behavior are so distressing that even the most hardened warrior needs the solace of moral, and perhaps sacred, structure.[7] The old adage "There are no atheists in foxholes" may have an element of truth, but that faith may not be a response to mortal fear; rather, to the need for reassurance that there is meaning in the struggle and strife, some moral order hidden in the experience of chaos and omnipresent moral calamity. It is just such meaning that Chaplain Rabbi Roland Gittelsohn brought to the survivors of Iwo Jima—and eventually, the nation—in his still quoted dedicatory sermon at the Fifth Marine Cemetery in 1945, "The Purest Democracy," which concludes, "We here solemnly swear: This shall not be in vain! Out of this, and from the suffering and sorrow of those who mourn this, will come—we promise—the birth of a new freedom for the sons of men everywhere."

One form of injury first recognized in twenty-first-century wars and now widely applied to the victims of any traumatic stress is post-traumatic stress disorder (PTSD). I believe the term is a misnomer. The profound response to the trauma need not be viewed as a disorder, but the perfectly healthy—albeit very difficult—struggle of an individual to integrate the dissonance within oneself generated by the traumatic experience. I further believe this is especially true when applied to wartime experiences. While I am admittedly a lone voice in preferring to reference PTSR, "post-traumatic stress response," there is a growing consensus that PTSD/R is often a consequence of moral injury. The U.S. Navy psychiatrist responsible for the response to PTSD/R within the U.S. Marine Corps, Dr. William

Nash, has long partnered with military chaplains to help marine and naval warriors respond to moral injury. Moral injury is the perception that the warriors' wartime actions violated the warriors' sense of morality. This dissonance between the warriors' personal sense of morality is exacerbated by the common mistranslation of the sixth commandment as "You shall not *kill*." Indeed, under the influence of this mistranslation, our larger society believes that the commandment prohibits all killing (including accidental homicide, self-defense, and in the minds of some, the killing of animals). Vice Admiral James Stockdale (a naval aviator who spent seven years as a POW in Vietnam) spoke of "the healing power" of discovering this mistranslation and learning that the commandment prohibited not killing but murder. Many combat veterans need moral and spiritual healing and the assurance that while they may have killed, they did not commit murder.

Meaningful ceremonies also can be vital tools in healing the wounded soul. In Numbers 31:19, Moses commands those returning from battle with the Midianites to "stay outside the camp seven days; every one among you . . . who has slain [not murdered] a person or touched a corpse shall purify himself." Today our rabbis in uniform, who harness the power of ceremony and ritual, help the returning warrior reenter the camp of civilian life. Rabbi and retired Colonel Bonnie Koppel developed services of welcome that specifically address moral injury for returning warriors. As a chaplain, I employed the rejuvenating power of mikveh, followed by a recitation of the *Gomeil* blessing the next Shabbat, appealing to "the One who doest good unto the undeserving, and who has dealt kindly with me," followed by the congregational response, "May the One who has shown you kindness deal unto thee every kindness." I found these combinations of divine and communal acceptance profoundly powerful in helping the warrior shed a sense of shame and distance from civilian community.

Finally, the rules themselves: the U.S. Department of Defense has developed a 1,193-page *Law of War Manual*, a legal compendium of all relevant U.S. laws and treaty obligations that is the basis of courses taught our troops throughout their career, commencing at basic training. For our purposes, the preface is most instructive. It somewhat inspirationally posits:

> The law of war is a part of our military heritage, and obeying it is the right thing to do. But we also know that the law of war poses no obstacle to fighting well and prevailing. . . For example, the self-control needed to refrain from violations of the law of war under the stresses of combat is the same good order and discipline necessary to operate cohesively and victoriously in battle.

That is a tall and optimistic order for a nineteen-year-old warrior to grasp and internalize, but still a vital lesson for every U.S. warrior. In very real terms, this is the U.S. government's response to one of our first questions: "If the cause is just, is it ethical to risk defeat by adhering to theoretical or perhaps aspirational 'laws' of war, or is 'all fair in love and war'?"

You might imagine that this adherence to a code of conduct is a luxury afforded only to the United States, a superpower incapable of imagining defeat. However, it is mirrored in the aspirational understanding of Israel's government and military. The Israel Defense Force's *Code of Ethics and Mission* is a succinct two pages. Amongst its thirteen statements of values we read, "The IDF servicemen and women will use their weapons and force only for the purpose of their mission, only to the necessary extent, and will maintain their humanity even during combat. IDF soldiers will not use their weapons and force to harm human beings who are not combatants or prisoners of war," and "IDF soldiers will be meticulous in giving only lawful orders, and shall refrain from obeying blatantly illegal orders."

Killing is a given in warfare. As long as we believe that nation-states have a right to send armed forces to war, *jus ad bellum*, warriors will kill and be killed. While that is, I believe, an intractable and hugely unfortunate, even pernicious, truth, I also believe that warriors need rules to distinguish justified killing, *jus in bello*, from murder. The rules assist them in overcoming the inevitable and profound emotional wounds of combat. The rules help confirm their understanding of themselves as moral individuals and their sense of personal self-worth. We at home, insulated as we are from the realities of combat and the fog of war, are ill equipped to write these rules. Rather, we ought to partner with experienced military leaders in refashioning the laws of war, as well as in healing those who suffer grievous emotional wounds from the wars in which they fought on our behalf, in our defense, and following our directions. Let us remember that in a democracy, we all bear responsibility for the action of our military.

Notes

1   In fact the quest to refine our understanding of "justice in warfare," *jus in bello*, continues in academia, in most militaries (including the American and Israeli), and in many other venues. Remarkably, the quest is often led by warriors in partnership with moral philosophers. The conversation is enriched by scholars, such as Professor Michael Walzer of the Institute for Advanced Studies at Princeton (I highly recommend his book *Just and Unjust Wars*, which is still relevant forty years after publication) and Professor Asa Kasher of Tel Aviv University, and by numerous papers and articles authored by experienced warriors at the Naval War College, Army War College, and National War College and found in almost every edition of military professional journals such as *Proceedings*.

2   Author's translation.

3   *Babylonian Talmud, Sanhedrin* 37a.

4   *Babylonian Talmud, Sanhedrin* 72a–b.

5   *Mishnah Makot* 1:10.

6   *Babylonian Talmud, Sanhedrin* 40b; Maimonides, *Mishneh Torah, Hilchot Sanhedrin* 12.

7   The unusually public response by senior U.S. military leaders to the presidential pardon of a U.S. Navy Seal and two U.S. Army officers convicted of a war crimes, including the forced resignation of the Secretary of the Navy and the revelations of the Seal's subordinates emotional testimony against him, demonstrate our warriors' determination to preserve the rules of war as intrinsic to their military ethos even in the face of political pressure (Reuters, 15 November, 2019; *New York Times*, 24 November, 2019; 30 November, 2019; 27 December, 2019).

Police Violence

Rabbi Jonathan Siger

ONE THING ABOUT police-involved shootings is that they tend to happen really quickly. Police officers have about a second and a half to get a sense of whether they are in danger, to draw their gun, and to get it on target.

If you're a police officer, by the time you see a gun pointed at you, you're already in big trouble. It takes less than half a second for someone holding a gun to turn it at an officer and pull the trigger. In a study entitled "Reasonableness and Reaction Time,"[1] psychologists found that even when the officer has a weapon drawn and pointed at a suspect, 61 percent of the time the officer fired at the same time or later than the assailant. This is because, as other studies have demonstrated, "action is always faster than reaction."

Police officers must be assertive and commanding in the face of uncertainty. Every traffic stop, every knock on the door of a house where a domestic disturbance has been reported, has the potential to end in injury or death. Detainees often fight arrest, especially while drunk or on drugs (or not on the right drugs), and angry people who feel they have nothing to lose are dangerous and unpredictable. Preservation of life is the police officer's first priority, and the life of the officer must come first. At the same time, instances of police misconduct, negligence, and incompetence have resulted in the wrongful deaths of too many people for a society committed to "justice for all" to ignore.

Preventing Blood Revenge

> Hillel, upon discovering a skull floating in a river, picked it up
> and spoke, "As you were a drowner, you were drowned, and
> your drowners shall be drowned."[2]

Many people (including Rabbi Hillel!) are predisposed to *lex talionis*,
the law of "eye for eye" (Leviticus 24:20). Murder leads to acts of
blood vengeance, resulting in a escalating cycle of violence and repri-
sals. Absent a governing force, chaos and disorder soon fill the void.

As explained in *M'chilta D'Rabbi Yishmael*,[3] the Ten Commandments were given on two tablets, each engraved with five divine
utterances. These commandments accordingly consist of pairs; "I
the Eternal am your God," at the top of the first tablet, is a coun-
terpart to "You shall not murder," at the top of the second. Just as
destroying a statue or picture of a king or queen would be considered
a crime against the honor of that king or queen, so too, destroying a
human being is a direct affront to the One in whose likeness humanity is made. To be sure, the damage of such destruction is more than
symbolic. According to the Mishnah, Creation culminated in a single human being in order to teach us that "the one who destroys a
human life . . . has destroyed the entire world, and whoever saves a
single life . . . has saved the entire world."[4] The quote is an impressive proof text for the immeasurable value of a human life—and the
greatness of the transgression in taking one.

This is not to say that taking of human life is always forbidden by
Jewish law; only the unlawful killing of a person is prohibited. The
Torah allows for degrees of homicide, and intent serves an important purpose in determining consequence. For example, if a person
working on a roof *accidentally* dropped a hammer on a coworker and
killed the person, the clumsy and unfortunate roofer would be given
the opportunity to flee to a "city of refuge," with the understanding
that if the family of the person killed ever catches the roofer outside of the sanctuary city, the family could avenge the death without
bloodguilt (see Numbers 35:10–28). Such leniency is not found in the
case of the intentional murderer. For one convicted of taking human

life with criminal intent, the only acceptable penalty was death (Numbers 35:16–21, 35:31): "When a man schemes against another and kills through treachery, you shall take that person from My very altar to be put to death" (Exodus 21:14). Nobody is above the law, and even the High Priest should be punished with death for murder should he be guilty of it.[5]

The Sages taught, "From where is it derived that with regard to one who pursues another in order to kill that person, the pursued party may be saved at the cost of the pursuer's life? The verse states: 'You shall not stand idly by the blood of another' (Leviticus 19:16)."[6] According to biblical and Rabbinic law, we don't just have an obligation to legally prosecute and punish those who murder in order to prevent a cycle of revenge killings. *We have an obligation to stop murders from happening by defending ourselves and others*, just as we must try to save someone from drowning. In order to preserve innocent life, we must do whatever it takes, even if it means killing an assailant.

A Rabbinic Distinction: Between Homicide and Murder

Ideally, one would be able to warn off attackers before a murder takes place or wound them in some way so as to stop the attack without taking their life, but there is no burden on the part of the intervening person to do so. An additional note is made by Rabbi Yonatan ben Shaul, who held that whenever one can stop an attacker by wounding without killing and chooses to kill instead, the wounder becomes a murderer. The Talmudic Sages in general do not put that burden on assigned watchmen, because would-be murderers or rapists should have no expectation of restraint from someone trying to stop them.[7] While there is no specific standard use of force policy shared by every law enforcement agency in the United States, there is a widely accepted continuum of force taught and practiced throughout the field. A gun should only be drawn if there exists an immediate or near-immediate need to shoot somebody, and only when the subject is assumed to carry a lethal force. Once a situation has risen to the level of lethal force in self-defense or in defense of human life, officers are not trained or expected to have the capacity or time to shoot the gun out of a robber's hand or shoot the leg of someone charging with a butcher knife. They are trained to shoot the biggest target, the "center of mass," which, with human beings, is the chest and upper abdomen. For those concerned with excessive police violence, more training in de-escalation techniques must be a priority within our agencies.

The Talmud discusses two verses from Exodus concerning home invasions and presents a contradiction: "If the thief is seized while tunneling and beaten to death, there is no bloodguilt in that case. If the sun had already risen, there is bloodguilt in that case" (Exodus 22:1–2). The Rabbis interpret the phrase "If the sun had already risen" beyond the biblical differentiation between a daytime versus nighttime home invasion. They read it as a metaphor: "If the matter is as 'clear as daylight' that the burglar is not coming to you intending no physical harm, but rather the intention is to kill you, arise and kill the burglar first. But if you are not sure about the intentions [if the burglar is, for example, your own father whom you can assume has no intention of killing you], do not kill the person."[8] It is the nature and right of people to defend their home from a nighttime invader with force, and any burglar breaking in should know as much. It may be that they accordingly expect to kill any victim who resists. The homeowner can kill the intruder based on the sense of being in deadly danger and thus is not a murderer. Furthermore, not only the homeowner, but also the neighbors are permitted to intercede and kill the burglar if there is a credible threat to human life. However, one is *not* allowed to kill a burglar if there is no reason to believe the person intends harm beyond theft (for example, in case the burglar turns out to be your own father, as in the hypothetical scenario presented in the Talmud). In conclusion, *in the case of a home invasion*, if there is the slightest doubt whether the burglar intends to do personal harm, the burglar is considered a *rodeif*, a murderous pursuer, "and the Torah states a principle: If someone comes to kill you, rise and kill him first."[9]

Killing someone to prevent rape, murder, or kidnapping is homicide. Killing someone in legitimate self-defense is homicide. The sixth commandment does not prohibit homicide—it prohibits intentional, unjust, and unwarranted homicide. *Lo tirtzach*, "You shall not murder," is not the same as *lo lamit*, "You shall not put to death," or *lo taharog*, "You shall not kill."

Between Mere Suspicion, Actual Threats, and Blood Revenge: Contemporary Police Violence

Regardless of moral, legal, or ethical justifications, very few people want to kill anybody, let alone strangers. Unfortunately, this is a possibility a police officer must be prepared for. In carrying out sworn service, their lives, the lives of their partners, and the lives of the citizens they interact with depend on their ability to defend against sudden deadly threats.

The best self-defense training includes stimulus-response conditioning. As Lt. Col. Dave Grossman explains in his book *On Killing*,[10] police academies don't teach future officers what to do in an emergency; instead, they condition their future officers to respond to a stimulus, so that when fear (or panic) overwhelms them, conditioning takes over and they react automatically and in the moment, doing what they have been conditioned to do. In a fire evacuation or an airplane engine failure, this saves lives. In a gunfight, it both saves and, unfortunately, takes them.

Current psychological research[11] by psychologists at the University of Toronto and Kent State University shows what anecdotal evidence has long suggested. Law enforcement officers are subject to the same moral distress, moral injury, resultant compassion fatigue, post-traumatic stress symptoms, and disorders that military combat veterans face. Compassion fatigue is a type of spiritual and/or psychological burnout resulting from direct exposure to trauma or secondary stress. Some degree of compassion fatigue is common among first responders, relief workers, and ER nurses. Anyone who regularly deals with trauma is at risk. It is not that the person suffering from severe compassion fatigue does not care anymore; it's that they can't care anymore. Left unchecked, in the context of policing, that fatigue makes an officer more likely to kill someone who is not a threat. Or, having developed the hypervigilance associated with PTSD, a merely suspicious subject triggers a fight response. The stimulus-response conditioning takes over, and in the time it takes to read this sentence, the shooting has happened.

In 2017, police shot and killed 987 people in America.[12] Of those killed, more than 300 were attempting to flee, and 68 were unarmed. A quarter of those killed were mentally ill. The number of white people shot and killed by police was far higher (457) than the number of black people (223). Proportionally to the demographics of our country, these numbers do not indicate a lack of racial bias. On the contrary, they demonstrate another facet of the imbalance. Black Americans are disproportionately shot by police, just as they are disproportionately stopped and searched, disproportionately prosecuted for crimes, and disproportionately incarcerated. And yet, where police violence toward citizens is concerned, a recent controversial study by Harvard professor Roland G. Fryer found that while Houston police were more likely to use nonlethal violence against black detainees, they were 20 percent less likely to employ their firearm in the encounter.[13]

Of course, not all police killings involve shooting. On July 17, 2014, Eric Garner was killed by what the medical examiner reported as "compression of neck, compression of chest and prone positioning during physical restraint by police."[14] The crime he was suspected of committing was selling single cigarettes without a tax stamp. The policeman who placed Garner in the chokehold while trying to restrain him was not indicted, prompting the United States Department of Justice to open its own investigation. When the DOJ investigation resulted in "no action," it drew strong protest from the Department of Justice's Civil Rights Division, which led to the removal of the FBI agents and the prosecutors in charge of that investigation. While New York City eventually settled the case with Mr. Garner's family for $5.9 million, others paid a far higher price. On December 20, 2014, following weeks of protests against police violence and a seeming lack of accountability, two NYPD officers were shot to death in an ambush by a man who had cited Garner's wrongful death as reason to kill police officers. On July 16, 2019, it was announced that the U.S. Department of Justice under the personal direction of Attorney General William Barr had declined to charge the officer with any civil rights violations.[15]

One would hope it goes without saying that revenge murder of police officers is not an appropriate or justifiable response to police misconduct or the failings of the justice system, especially when random police officers are targeted in retaliation for the actions of others. This results only in more deaths and a deeper mistrust of potential subjects by police. For their part, the police must not be treated as if they function above the law and must work against any perception that they believe they do. Even the High Priest can be prosecuted for murder. It serves neither law enforcement nor the community they are sworn to protect when tribalism rules the day; one of the main sources of "moral distress" among police officers is bearing witness to a colleague's abuse of their position and not being able to speak out, let alone stop it, for fear of losing their job or social standing in the law enforcement community.

In discussing the case of the home invasion, the Sages of the Talmud use the normative love of a parent for their child as a standard for compassion.[16] Police are by necessity called upon to act as parents do: they are called to protect us and serve our needs. They defend us from danger, including the danger that we sometimes pose to ourselves. They enforce rules and can use force when necessary to ensure our compliance with the law. And just as with parents, there is a line where discipline becomes abuse, where negligence becomes criminal, and where lack of compassion breaches the sacred trust that is the very heart of the relationship. For this reason, we must ensure that our police officers have the training, support, and professional resources needed to prevent compassion fatigue. They cannot do the job we ask of them otherwise.

Jewish Responsibility and the Contemporary Problem of Police Violence

For most of Jewish history, Jews have lived as subjects of foreign powers or as a disenfranchised minority. As such, discussions of Jewish police power or the conduct of a Jewish government were either nostalgic fantasy or theoretical speculation. Not so today, where as Americans, we have not just a voice but a responsibility to participate in our government. As such, the conduct of police officers and the consequences of their actions are very much our concern, and we have an obligation to ensure the highest standards of training, support, and oversight.

Notes

1 J. Pete Blair et al., "Reasonableness and Reaction Time," *Police Quarterly* 14, no. 4 (2011): 323–43.

2 *Mishnah Avot* 2:6.

3 *M'chilta D'Rabbi Yishmael* 20:14, trans. Shraga Silverstein.

4 *Mishnah Sanhedrin* 4:5.

5 *M'chilta D'Rabbi Yishmael* 2:14.

6 *Babylonian Talmud, Sanhedrin* 73a.

7 *Babylonian Talmud, Sanhedrin* 74a.

8 *Babylonian Talmud, Sanhedrin* 72a.

9 *Babylonian Talmud, Sanhedrin* 72a.

10 Dave Grossman, *On Killing: The Psychological Cost of Learning to Kill in War and Society* (Boston: Little, Brown, 1996).

11 Konstantinos Papazoglou and Brian Chopko, "The Role of Moral Suffering (Moral Distress and Moral Injury) in Police Compassion Fatigue and PTSD: An Unexplored Topic," *Frontiers in Psychology* 8 (1999): 2017.

12 "Police Shootings Database," *Washington Post*, accessed June 30, 2018, https://www.washingtonpost.com/graphics/2018/national/police-shootings-2018/.

13 Roland G. Fryer Jr., "An Empirical Analysis of Racial Differences in Police Use of Force," Harvard University, July 2017, https://scholar.harvard.edu/files/fryer/files/empirical_analysis_tables_figures.pdf.

14 Giri Nathan, "Eric Garner Died from Chokehold While in Police Custody," *Time*, August 1, 2014, https://time.com/3071288/eric-garner-chokehold-death-nypd-medical-examiner/.

15 Emily Saul and Lia Eustachewich, "AG Barr Made Decision to Not Bring

Charges against Eric Garner Cop: Official," *New York Post*, July 16, 2019, https://nypost.com/2019/07/16/ag-barr-made-decision-to-not-bring-charges-against-eric-garner-cop-official/.

16 *Babylonian Talmud, Sanhedrin* 72a.

Seventh Commandment

לֹא תִּנְאָף

You shall not commit adultery.
—Exodus 20:13

Feminist Reading of the Commandment

Rabbi Darcie Crystal

"You shall not commit adultery" (Exodus 20:13). Included in the Ten Commandments between the prohibitions of murder and stealing, this commandment confronts us with the question of contemporary relevance in the context of twenty-first-century social and sexual mores.

As a rabbi, I have witnessed the destructive toll adulterous relationships can take on the individuals involved, their families, and their communities. Our tradition's prohibition against adultery takes on particular weight and poignancy in the context of our society's continuous reevaluation of the relationship between sex, power, and authority.

In this essay, I first explore the commandment's function in its biblical and Rabbinic contexts. Then, I shift the focus from perpetrator to victim, before returning to the importance of the commandment for contemporary Jewish communal life and the life of broader society.

While I take the commandment prohibiting adultery as a starting point, I broaden the discussion to include other topics of sexual ethics that are playing out in today's society, among those the necessity of consent and the danger of abuse of power.

Traditional Approaches to Adultery in Jewish Texts

Let's begin by understanding the commandment within its biblical context. In Genesis 20:9, adultery is referred to as "a great sin" (*chataah g'dolah*), a term taken from ancient Near Eastern legal contracts, where that phrase refers solely to adultery.[1] The term is a first indication that adultery was viewed as one of the most sinful acts one could commit.

In the Ten Commandments, adultery is listed as the second of three major prohibitions: murder, adultery, and stealing. The commandment is stated in the absolute—*lo tinaf*, "do not commit adultery"—and not as a conditional (*if you violate X, the punishment is Y*). Committing adultery, stealing, and murder "are not only illegal; they are wrong. They not only disrupt society; they violate universal principles. Furthermore, the Decalogue enshrines a fundamental principal of Judaism: How we treat one another is of concern to God."[2] As this is an offense not simply between humans but between the sinners and God, a man could neither offer pardon to his wife or her lover, nor mitigate the punishment, a privilege he would have had in other ancient Near Eastern law codes.[3]

Within the Decalogue, adultery refers specifically to a married woman who had sexual intercourse with another man.[4] Polygamy was a common practice in the ancient Near East, but only for men. In the context of this patriarchal society, although "a husband had an exclusive right to his wife, a wife might share her husband with his other wives and did not have an exclusive right to him."[5] Despite the seeming inequality inherent in the Exodus commandment, in Leviticus 20:10 the penalty for adultery *for both men and women* was death: "If a man commits adultery with a married woman, committing adultery with another man's wife, the adulterer and the adulteress shall be put to death." The severity of the punishment reinforces the impression that adultery was perceived not simply as a violation of a human contract, but also as an offense against God.

Throughout the Books of Prophets, God is offended whenever the Israelites stray from their worship, as if they are adulterous. For example, Ezekiel chastises the Israelites for their idolatrous ways, telling them, "In your insatiable lust you also played the whore with the Assyrians; you played the whore with them, but were still unsated. . . . [You were like] the adulterous wife who welcomes strangers instead of her husband" (Ezekiel 16:28, 32).

In the Book of Malachi, we see that God takes adultery as a personal affront: "The Eternal is a witness between you and the wife of your youth with whom you have broken faith, though she is your partner and covenanted spouse. Did not the One make [all,] so that all remaining life-breath is God's? And what does that One seek but godly folk? So be careful of your life-breath, and let no one break faith with the wife of his youth" (Malachi 2:14–15). Breaking the covenant of marriage was as offensive to God as it was to the spouse. God is invested in that human relationship.

The Rabbis subscribed to this view as well. The Rabbinic term for marriage is *kiddushin*, which comes from the Hebrew word for "holy." To this day, we call the Jewish wedding ceremony *kiddushin*, "a process of making [a relationship] holy." The Talmud declares that regardless of any pressure from inside or outside your community, you should give up your life before engaging in idolatry, incest, or adultery.[6] Within a tradition that places the highest value on the preservation of life, the Rabbis still arrived at the extraordinary judgment that marital responsibilities take precedence over life itself.

Much of the Rabbinic legal tradition around adultery is focused, perhaps obsessively so, on paternity and legitimacy; a child born outside of marriage was seen as illegitimate. Even in a matrilineal society, paternal descent was essential to defining membership: both the lines of the *kohanim* ("priests") and *l'viyim* ("Levites"), who used to have important ceremonial roles in the Temple and continued to have certain privileges and duties in Rabbinic liturgy and ritual, were transmitted through the father.

In the Bible, the punishment for adultery was death by stoning, a form of capital punishment reserved for acts that threatened the well-being of the entire nation. "Punishment by stoning enabled the entire public to participate and thereby express its outrage against the crime and the threat it posed to God's authority and society's welfare."[7] The Rabbis upheld the death penalty for adultery, because imposing harsh punishments for perpetrators of illicit sexual activity was seen as an effective strategy for maintaining and enforcing communal cohesion.

The Rabbis' main concern regarding adultery was its potentially destructive impact on the larger community. Similar concerns might move us in our own age.

Adultery in the Contemporary Context

We know that sexual ethics represents a far broader category than adultery; our contemporary culture has shifted the conversation to focus on issues around consent and abuse of power, with movements like #MeToo centering the voices of those victimized.

It is clear that American views on sexual ethics have radically shifted. The Reform Movement is deeply engaged in these conversations. We support LGBTQ relationships, covenants, and marriages; single individuals who seek to have children; single parents; and those who choose to adopt. At the same time, most of us are not particularly concerned with the status of the priestly line, passed down by the father. We are egalitarian in our approach to liturgical and ritual matters.

While America's culture shifts from its puritanical roots to openness, equality, and inclusion, we also become increasingly aware of the diversity of marital and other romantic commitments. One out of six Americans report having sex with someone other than their spouse while married.[8] Though this number might make us wonder whether we should simply dismiss our previous approach to the seventh commandment, I would argue that the prohibition of adultery should still hold power for us today. Two dynamics make this commandment relevant: an often terrible imbalance of power between the two people who have engaged in extramarital relations; and that such an affair impacts not only those directly involved, their spouses, and their children, but their entire communities. When a married person engages in a sexual relationship outside of their marriage, the sacred trust between those spouses is broken. But that violation of trust extends well beyond the two involved in the affair; their children and maybe even other members of their communities may find it difficult to trust those individuals.

In the Talmud, the Rabbis teach:

> There was a certain Torah scholar who gained a bad reputation due to rumors about his conduct. Rav Yehudah said, "What should be done? To excommunicate him is not an option. The Sages need him, as he is a great Torah authority. Not to excommunicate him is also not an option, as then the name of heaven would be desecrated."[9]

Already in the Talmud the damage that can occur when a respected leader of the community engages in immoral behavior is fully acknowledged.

Today, the Central Conference of American Rabbis recognizes the importance of holding its rabbis to high ethical standards in many areas, among them sexual boundaries. Section V of the CCAR Ethics Code[10] states:

> As rabbis, Jewish leaders, and pastoral guides we are commanded to exemplify holiness through our teachings and our lives. We bear the greatest responsibility for ensuring that ethical and sexual boundaries are scrupulously respected in all our relationships with the men, women, and young people who turn to us in trust. Sexual misconduct by rabbis is a sin against human beings; it is also a *Chilul Hashem* (profanation of God's name).

The CCAR prohibits any sexual or emotional abuse and encourages rabbis to bear in mind the sacred nature of the responsibility that comes with their title.

The CCAR Ethics Code continues:

> As rabbis vested with real and symbolic religious authority, we have the responsibility to recognize the vulnerability of those whom we teach, counsel, and serve. It is our obligation to maintain appropriate boundaries in all situations and settings. . . . Any such act or behavior, even if it appears to be consensual, which exploits the vulnerability of another, compromises the moral integrity of the rabbi and is an ethical violation.

Both of these excerpts point to the importance of recognizing that the power imbalance between a clergyperson and a layperson (whether congregant, staff member, or even someone outside of that rabbi's professional community) can create a dangerous dynamic in a relationship, particularly when this relationship is adulterous. Though this power imbalance could become an issue even within a consensual relationship between two single adults (one of whom is a clergy member), there are certainly healthy relationships between clergy and laypeople.

While it is not surprising that a rabbinical organization like the CCAR grounds its policies in Jewish tradition and values the biblical prohibition against adultery, it is perhaps more surprising that many secular institutions—in business, public service, the military, and medical fields—do so as well. Because of numerous cases of married executives becoming romantically involved with their subordinates, those institutions have expanded their anti-harassment and anti-discrimination policies to include restrictions on "fraternization," proscribing relationships with subordinates under any circumstances. In recent years, the married CEOs from corporations ranging from Best Buy to Intel have lost their positions under these policies. Universities have instituted similar policies prohibiting relationships between its faculty and students, reflecting their conclusion that when there is an imbalance of power and authority, there is always a question of consent.

In the U.S. military's code of conduct, adultery is prosecuted under article 134, also known as the "General Article." This article "prohibits conduct which is of a nature to bring discredit upon the armed forces, or conduct which is prejudicial to good order and discipline." Under the Unified Code of Military Justice (UCMJ) and its *Manual for Courts-Martial*, "adultery is a crime with punishments as severe as dishonorable discharge, loss of all benefits (including pension), and even a year in jail."[11] Inherent in this code is the acknowledgment that an affair between one of higher and lower rank can compromise the integrity of the unit or worse, the larger branch of the military.

The APA Ethical Principles of Psychologists and Code of Conduct, like the codes of all major mental health organizations, prohibits sexual involvements between therapists and their clients: "Harm is so likely to occur, and autonomy so likely to be compromised in the therapy relationship, that the code establishes an absolute prohibition against sexual relationships."[12] Additionally, the code strictly prohibits any sexual involvement between therapist and client for two years post-termination of the client relationship.

These policies underscore the fundamental wisdom of Jewish tradition: adultery is not only a matter between two individuals; it can compromise the integrity of an entire community. Megan Barry,[13] the former mayor of Nashville and a rising star in the Democratic Party, resigned from her position in 2018 when it came to light that she had an affair with her former head of security. He was paid overtime while the city paid for the couple to attend evening concerts, yoga classes, and business trips, all under the guise of city business. She broke the trust of her husband and her constituents, and she broke the law, leaving her city scrambling to recover and learn to trust a new leader.[14] Often, issues of sexual and financial misconduct become intertwined—given the proximity of the prohibitions of stealing and adultery in the biblical context, perhaps this should not come as a surprise!

Conclusion

Rabbi Lord Jonathan Sacks explains:

> When a society loses faith, eventually it loses the very idea of a sexual ethic, and the result in the long term is violence and the exploitation of the powerless by the powerful. . . . There is a breakdown of trust where it matters most. So it was in the days of the patriarchs. Sadly, so it is today. Judaism, by contrast, is the sanctification of relationship, the love between husband and wife which is as close as we will ever get to understanding God's love for us.[15]

The ripple effect of a seemingly entirely "private" affair can cause tremendous pain and damage to many people both close to the couple and in their broader community. While we no longer practice stoning, the punishment for this violation can still be harsh: communal opprobrium, loss of job and professional credentials, divorce, and even (when combined with other crimes) incarceration. And the path back to "wholeness," the "turning back" (*t'shuvah*) is extremely difficult. It takes immense work and time to earn back the trust of those victims who were violated and to rebuild the integrity of the entire system that makes a community function.

NOTES

1   *Etz Hayim: Torah and Commentary*, ed. David L. Lieber (New York: Rabbinical Assembly, 2001), *p'shat* commentary on Exodus 32:21, 534.
2   *Etz Hayim*, *d'rash* commentary on Exodus 20:1–14, 441.
3   *Etz Hayim*, *p'shat* commentary on Deuteronomy 5:17, 1021.
4   *Etz Hayim*, *p'shat* commentary on Exodus 20:13, 447.
5   *Etz Hayim*, *p'shat* commentary on Deuteronomy 5:17, 1021.
6   *Babylonian Talmud, Sanhedrin* 74a.
7   *Etz Hayim*, *p'shat* commentary on Deuteronomy 13:11, 1070.
8   Wendy Wang, "Who Cheats More? The Demographics of Infidelity in America" *IFS Blog*, Institute for Family Studies, January 10, 2018, https://ifstudies.org/blog/who-cheats-more-the-demographics-of-cheating-in-america.
9   *Babylonian Talmud, Mo-eid Katan* 17a.
10 The Central Conference of American Rabbis is the professional body that brings together Reform rabbis throughout North America. In order to be a member of this organization, each rabbi agrees to abide by the Code of Ethics, an ecclesiastical (as opposed to a legal) document that outlines standards of behavior for rabbis of the Reform Movement. The CCAR Ethics Committee is charged with assessing and adjudicating allegations of violations of the Code of Ethics.
11 "The David Petraeus Affair: Why the U.S. Military Outlaws Adultery," *The Week*, November 15, 2012, https://theweek.com/articles/470371/davidpetraeusaffair-why-military-outlaws-adultery.
12 Stephen Behnke, "Sexual Involvement with Former Clients: A Delicate Balance of Core Values," *Monitor on Psychology* 35, no. 11 (December 2004): 76, https://www.apa.org/monitor/dec04/ethics.
13 Quite obviously, both men and women in positions of authority can engage in damaging relationships with a subordinate.
14 Nate Rau and Joey Garrison, "Nine Months after Megan Barry Resignation, Nashville Leaders Still Struggle to Rebuild Public Trust," *Tennessean*,

December 28, 2018, https://www.tennessean.com/story/news/2018/12/28/nashville-mayor-megan-barry-affair-resignation-top-story-2018/2389807002/.

15 Rabbi Jonathan Sacks, "What Is the Theme of the Stories of Genesis?," *Covenant & Conversation* (blog), Office of Rabbi Sacks, December 19, 2016, http://rabbisacks.org/theme-stories-genesis-vayeshev-5777/.

Adultery and Deception

RABBI ELIANA FISCHEL

THE 2004 CHRISTMAS CLASSIC *Love Actually* exemplifies assumed limits of adultery.[1] The movie follows the lives of eight couples during the month before Christmas as they navigate the complexities of love, intimacy, communication, and heartbreak. One of the couples, Harry (Alan Rickman) and Karen (Emma Thompson), begin the film embodying the ideal relationship—married, children, a witty banter, and a lot of love. That is until Mia (Heike Makatsch), Harry's new secretary, begins a flirtatious relationship with the otherwise faithful man. Their flirtations increase throughout the movie, until, in the most heart-wrenching scene of the film, Harry buys Mia a gold necklace that Karen finds in his coat pocket. On Christmas Eve, Karen opens her present from Harry, thinking it is the necklace, only to discover a Joni Mitchell album. Karen understands that the gold necklace has gone to someone else. She understands, for the first time, that her husband has another woman in his life.

It is unclear whether Harry and Mia had sex. The movie intimates that they did; however, it only makes *explicit* the deception of the gift exchange. This emphasis of the movie makes a clear point: the act of sex is not the whole story in the world of relational deception. Whether or not Harry and Mia had sex, Harry was dishonest. Harry put a (literal) higher price on his secretary than on his wife. Harry and Karen's relationship would never be the same. Was what Harry did wrong? Most of us would probably say yes. Was what Harry did adultery? Probably not, and in the biblical sense, not even close.

This essay will look at the seventh commandment, the prohibition of adultery (Exodus 20:13), and ask how the paradigm of adultery works, or does not work, for relationships today. First, we will look at the seventh commandment as it was originally intended and the ways in which that original intention creates problems today. We will explore how the term "adultery" could implicate other types of relational transgressions, other forms of adulterated deception. Finally, we will conclude with examples from peripheral modern communities that provide alternative answers to the question of adulterated deception.

Biblical and Historical Adultery

To understand the biblical definition of adultery, we need to understand biblical marriage. Biblical marriage was an economic acquisition. A man would pay a bride price, a *mohar*, for a given woman, thus transferring that woman from her father's economic holdings to her new husband's economic holdings (Genesis 34:12; Exodus 22:16; I Samuel 18:25). Lest this concept surprise us, we need to look no further than the stories of our Patriarchs, particularly of Jacob and his wives, to see how biblical marriage is part of property law (Genesis 29). Jacob offers Laban, Rachel's father, seven years of service for Rachel. Laban agrees. Seven years pass, and Laban deceptively gives Jacob not *Rachel*, but *Leah*. As readers, we cringe when Jacob realizes the deception. We cringe as romantics, but also as capitalists. Jacob worked for seven years toward a certain goal, toward a certain reward, toward a certain economic acquisition. His *work* was in vain.

Since biblical marriage was an economic acquisition, polygamy was the norm in biblical times: the richer a man was, the more wives and concubines he had. There was no richer man than King Solomon, who had seven hundred royal wives and three hundred concubines (I Kings 11:3). These women are listed as part of King Solomon's economic assets. King Solomon could not have been interested in loving or even procreating with each of these women. Rather, they were part of his household, demonstrating his wealth to other rulers.

Understanding biblical marriage as an economic and polygamous enterprise helps to put biblical adultery into perspective. The biblical prohibition against adultery has little to do with love and everything to do with property. As Rashi explains, the seventh commandment only applied to men having sexual relations with *married* women.[2] Married women were the property of their husbands. A man, whether he was married or not, who had sex with a married woman figuratively stole from her husband. The transgression is not one of breaking a covenantal relationship, but rather of theft. The actual prohibition against theft immediately follows the prohibition against adultery (Exodus 20:13), and in Proverbs 6:29 adultery is compared to the act of stealing, implicating that the two commandments share a common thread.

Furthermore, while the prohibition of adultery mandates a woman's sexual exclusivity, such a restriction is not placed on her husband. We can see this unilateral restriction in the stories of our Patriarchs. Abraham had three wives: Sarah, Hagar, and Keturah (Genesis 16:1, 16:3, 25:1). Jacob had two wives and two concubines: Leah, Rachel, Bilhah, and Zilpah (Genesis 29:23, 28 and 30:4, 9). Moses, the receiver of the commandments, had two wives: Zipporah and the unnamed Cushite woman (Exodus 2:21; Numbers 12:1). Clearly, the prohibition of adultery did not prohibit a man from sexual relations with other women.

Rabbinic Judaism reified and ritualized this relationship by introducing the ceremony of *kiddushin* (sanctification of marriage as represented by a change in status from daughter to wife) and *ketubah* (a contractual document that provides for a wife in the event of divorce or widowhood). Both *kiddushin* and *ketubah* mandate *female* sexual exclusivity but place minimal to no restrictions on the male partner. Once again, the male partner was free to have sexual relations with whomever he would like; the commandment against adultery did not apply to him.

If biblical and Rabbinic adultery only restricted the sexual "theft" of a woman, how did we get to the cringe-worthy moment of Karen discovering the gold necklace intended for Mia, thus possibly ending Karen and Harry's relationship? How did our conception of marriage, sex, and sexual exclusivity change so drastically?

Those answers originate in the Middle Ages, when two famous

rulings banned polygamy, thus restricting male sexual activity. Rabbeinu Gershom banned bigamy in his famous *takanah* of 1000 CE,[3] and Maimonides banned concubinage relationships in 1180 CE.[4] While some Jewish communities continued the practice of polygamy into the twentieth century,[5] by 1200 CE most Jewish marriages were between two individuals, and male sexual exclusivity was presumed.

Early American law, however, shows how legal definitions of adultery continued the concept of a marital "property law." Civil law prohibiting adultery is a remnant of American Puritan origins. When the Puritans arrived to this country, they determined that adultery with a *married* woman was a capital offense.[6] As states formed, prohibitions of adultery were written as both civil and criminal law, with and without gender restrictions.[7] Today, most states have abolished these laws. However, some states still have adultery laws, even if they are hardly used to prosecute adulterers.[8]

The Issues with Modern Adultery

Most Americans are surprised to discover that their cheating spouse could be fined fifty dollars or jailed for up to sixty days for the crime of having sex with another partner.[9] This sense of surprise is due, probably, to the fact that most Americans—including American Jews!—have divorced marriage and adultery from property law. By the end of the twentieth century, some Jewish feminist scholars had come out against Jewish marriage altogether because of its origins in property law.[10] Most Jews have not rejected the institution of Jewish marriage; they have simply amended the marriage ritual to be more inclusive. The same is true of adultery.

Contemporary legal definitions of adultery have extended the law to incorporate all genders. Both men and women are expected to stay sexually exclusive to their spouses—a custom that aims to sanctify the marital relationship. Unfortunately, this presumption has proved to be unsuccessful. In a 2012 *Washington Post* article, Eric Anderson reported that between 25 percent and 72 percent of married men cheat on their spouse, the discrepancy in the number owing to the fact that adultery is hard to report.[11] These numbers suggest that sexual exclusivity may be a good goal for marital relationships, but the presumption that all marital relationships are, indeed, sexually exclusive is flawed.

Furthermore, the issue of adultery does not seem to be the act of sex with another person. In 2015, a Gallup poll revealed that only 8 percent of Americans believe adultery to be morally acceptable, while 16 percent of Americans believe polygamy to be morally acceptable.[12] Since polygamy necessarily implies that a person has sex with multiple individuals, the moral issue with adultery must lie beyond the actual number of sexual partners. What is it, then, about adultery that Americans find so much more reprehensible?

A Focus on Adulterated Deception

Since we no longer view marriage as an act of economic acquisition, and since the presumption of mutual sexual exclusivity is being frequently transgressed, we might wonder whether the prohibition of adultery is still useful for today's relationships. A verse from Job provides a first possibility for reflection: "The eyes of the adulterer watch for twilight, thinking, 'No one will glimpse me then.' He masks his face" (Job 24:15). The adulterer goes through great lengths to be unseen. He goes into the dark—a time that connotes danger and murky behavior. He explicitly acts to trick those around him. He masks his face, not revealing who he is to those he loves. He deceives before he ever touches another person.

I propose that these acts of deception, acts that are murky and complicated but will clearly result in pain, are the transgressions that must be included within a modern understanding of the seventh commandment. The sin of adultery begins long before two people have sex. These are the sins of deception: trickery, lying, not telling the whole truth, and hiding one's self. These are the sins we need to combat in modern relationships, in addition to sexual infidelity. To do so, we may need to look to other types of relationships that focus on *these* transgressions, and not sexual promiscuity, as the ultimate relational sins.

An Answer from an Unlikely Source

Looking to the polyamory community for an answer to adultery could be seen as *asur*, as "forbidden"—as forbidden as beginning a chapter in a Jewish book on the Ten Commandments with a Christmas movie. Polyamorous relationships are defined as "consensual and emotionally intimate non-monogamous relationships in which both women and men can negotiate to have multiple partners."[13] Polyamorous communities highly value transparent communication, the key in combatting deception. Healthy polyamorous relationships begin with a negotiation period in which each party communicates what he or she needs. Susan Dominus, writing for the *New York Times Magazine*, explains this process of negotiation as she differentiates between polyamory and monogamy:

> Monogamy is an approach to relationships built on one bright-line rule: no sex with anyone else. Open relationships may sound like the more unfettered choice, but the first thing non-monogamous couples often do is draw up a list of guidelines: rules about protection, about the number of days a week set aside for dates, about how much information to share. Some spouses do not want to know any details about the other spouse's extramarital sex, while for others, those stories are a thrilling side benefit of the arrangement.[14]

Since sexual exclusivity is not presumed in polyamorous relationships, individuals must communicate their own expectations for a given relationship. These expectations aim to mitigate deception. They aim to prevent a problem before it occurs.

Questions for the Future of Un-adulterated, Deception-Free Relationships

What would relationships look like, monogamous or not, if the presumption was not sexual exclusivity but rather a deception-free relationship? What type of conversations would have to take place? Could we bring ourselves to ask our partners, "What would you like me to do if I become attracted to another person?" Could we challenge ourselves to ask our partners, "What would you like me to do if I become unsatisfied with parts of our relationship?" These questions are difficult and scary, yet they are the questions that could prevent the types of deception that we see in relationships each and every day.

At the end of *Love Actually*, the viewer does not know whether Karen and Harry are still together. They awkwardly greet each other at the airport and walk off with their children. If they do remain together, one can imagine that they have had some difficult conversations in order to keep their relationship alive. Those difficult conversations could take place at the beginning of a relationship. It is exponentially harder to have them once someone has already transgressed a relational boundary. Creating a history of open communication in good times provides a rubric for how to act when times get difficult. Asking the toughest of questions can be a great defense against adulterated deception. Asking the toughest of questions can assist in creating the holy covenantal relationships we espouse in our tradition.

NOTES

1 Richard Curtis et al., *Love Actually* (Universal Studios, 2004).
2 Rashi on Exodus 20:13.
3 *Shulchan Aruch, Even HaEizer* 1:10.
4 Maimonides, *Mishneh Torah, Hilchot M'lachim* 4:4.
5 There are some communities, particularly in Yemen and among Yemeni immigrants, who continue to practice polygamy or did so until the twentieth century. See David Sedley, "In Defiance of Israeli Law, Polygamy Sanctioned by Top Rabbis," Times of Israel, December 27, 2016, https://www.timesofisrael.com/in-defiance-of-israeli-law-polygamy-sanctioned-by-top-rabbis/.
6 Alyssa Miller, "Punishing Passion: A Comparative Analysis of Adultery Laws in the United States of America and Taiwan and Their Effects on Women," *Fordham International Law Journal* 41, no. 2 (2018): 425–36.
7 Miller, "Punishing Passion."
8 Jolie Lee, "In Which States Is Cheating on Your Spouse Illegal?," *Detroit Free Press*, April 17, 2014, https://www.freep.com/story/life/family/2014/04/17/in-which-states-is-cheating-on-your-spouse-illegal/28936155/.
9 Lee, "In Which States . . .?"
10 Rachel Adler, *Engendering Judaism* (Philadelphia: Jewish Publication Society, 1998), 172.

11 Eric Anderson, "Five Myths about Cheating," *Washington Post*, February 13, 2012, https://www.washingtonpost.com/opinions/five-myths-about-cheating/2012/02/08/gIQANGdaBR_story.html?utm_term=.3672fd19b6d9.

12 Andrew Dugan, "Once Taboo, Some Behaviors Now More Acceptable in U.S.," Gallup, June 1, 2015, https://news.gallup.com/poll/183455/once-taboo-behaviors-acceptable.aspx.

13 Elisabeth Sheff, *The Polyamorists Next Door: Inside Multiple Partner Relationships and Families* (New York: Rowman & Littlefield, 2015), x.

14 Susan Dominus, "Is an Open Marriage a Happier Marriage?," *New York Times Magazine*, May 11, 2017, www.nytimes.com/2017/05/11/magazine/is-an-open-marriage-a-happier-marriage.html?_r=0.

EIGHTH COMMANDMENT

לֹא תִגְנֹב

You shall not steal.
—Exodus 20:13

The Bible, Intellectual Property, and Authorship Integrity

ROBERTA ROSENTHAL KWALL, JD

IN 1982, SCULPTOR Frederick Hart completed the renowned work *Ex Nihilo*, the product of a thirteen-year spiritual quest preceding his conversion to Catholicism.[1] It depicts the creation of humankind out of the torrential void and was placed in the Washington National Cathedral.

Sadly for Hart, Warner Brothers featured a near-exact duplicate of the sculpture in the movie *The Devil's Advocate*, which formed the backdrop for a scene in which the main character encourages his children to participate in an incestuous relationship as the carved bodies of the sculpture come alive and grope one another in an erotic manner.[2] Hart ultimately received a favorable settlement from Warner Brothers that required changes in portions of the film to eliminate any perceived confusion in the future distribution of the movie. But his agony was tellingly revealed in his narrative of pain when he observed, "I feel absolutely outraged that a work that was meant to express the great majesty and beauty and mystery of God's creation has been radically perverted."[3]

The act of creation entails an infusion of the creator's mind, heart, and soul into the work. Many authors of creative works of all types maintain a certain type of relationship with their artistic "children." Given the highly personalized nature of creative authorship, this relationship is unique among other types of human production. In the majority of countries around the world, this relationship is protected by the legal doctrine known as *moral rights*, which safeguards an author's right to attribution and maintains the integrity of the work by preventing unauthorized changes that distort a work's meaning and message. When someone other than the author engages in behavior that alters a work's intended meaning and message or uses the work in a context that violates the author's vision and sensibilities, this conduct should be understood as a form of stealing the author's work. Of course the same can be said for violating an author's *copyright*, an area of law that has become increasingly prominent in our technology-rich environment.

Copyright law differs from moral rights in that copyright protects an author's *economic rights* to the work such as the rights to reproduce, display, perform, and distribute the protected work, as well as the right to create new works based on the original. In contrast, moral rights protect *the author's personal interests* that are distinct from the monetary realm. Moral rights protect the author's desired attribution interest, as well as the original conception of the work. Its focus is on the author's subjective vision. The author's *meaning* defines "what the work stands for" on an internal level, personal to the author. The author's *message* is what the author is intending to communicate externally on a more universal level.

Both copyright and moral rights violations could be considered within the scope of the eighth commandment, but here I focus on theft of the author's *personal* interests in the work ("a violation of the author's moral rights"). Theft in economic terms is a familiar concept, and the origins and application of Jewish law as it pertains to copyright jurisprudence have already been treated elsewhere.[4] Additionally, in the United States, copyright protection is a robust and well-known concept among the general population. In contrast, the idea of stealing an author's personal interests in the work is less known, largely because American law in this area lags well behind most of the rest of the world.[5] The copyright narrative in the United States is steeped in an economic framework emphasizing the sale and distribution of intellectual works. A perspective focusing on the internal and spiritual dimensions of creative enterprise is largely lacking, resulting in insufficient protections for authors' moral rights. Further, the story of the Jewish roots for this type of protection is largely unknown.

The Creation narratives found in Genesis are the most celebrated stories about creativity in Western society. Interestingly, when Frederick Hart began the process of creating *Ex Nihilo*, he consulted these narratives as resources for his own creative endeavor.[6] Genesis 1:27 states that "God created the human beings in [the divine] image." Historian and former librarian of Congress Daniel Boorstin credits this language with leading people to regard themselves as potential creators, underscoring an unprecedented parallel between God and humanity.[7] Rabbi Joseph Soloveitchik regards the Creation narratives in Genesis as "challenging man to create, to transform wilderness into productive life."[8]

The word "create" is derived from the Latin verb *creo*, meaning "to give birth to."[9] Rabbi Karyn Kedar writes that the opening verses of Genesis reveal a description of the womb: "The deep, unformed darkness is the womb, ripe with potential . . . the water is the amniotic waters that protect the fragility of life."[10] The idea that authors "give birth" to their artistic creations, known as *the parental metaphor of authorship*, provides the foundation for the insurmountable connection between authors and their work. This metaphor also defines stealing in the context of authorship. As early as 1710, Daniel Defoe referred to literary theft as a type of "child snatching."[11] Also, the word "plagiarism" is derived from the Latin term for "kidnapping."[12]

The attribution and integrity interests that are at the core of the moral rights doctrine have strong roots in Jewish tradition. In fact, a lack of regard for these interests was the cause of the first sin committed in the Garden of Eden. In Genesis 2:17, God commands Adam not to *eat* from the Tree of All Knowledge. But in Genesis 3:3, Eve tells the serpent that she may not eat the fruit, nor *touch* it, lest she die. A midrash tells us that in response, the serpent shoved Eve against the fruit and then said to her, "See, you did not die."[13] As she saw that she did not die from touching the fruit, the serpent was able to convince her that it would be just fine for her to eat the fruit as well.

But how was the serpent able to do this? The midrash explains that Adam wanted to add a safeguard for the commandment of not eating the fruit.[14] For that reason, he said not to even *touch* it. However, Adam did not tell Eve that the commandment not to touch the fruit was his own innovation. Adam let Eve think that this instruction came directly from God. By modifying God's original statement and not correctly identifying God's command and his own addition, Adam caused the expulsion from Eden.

This biblical narrative presents what may be the earliest recorded example of a violation of both attribution and integrity interests. Adam violated God's right of attribution by misattributing to God words that God did not speak (specifically, the injunction not to touch the fruit). Adam also violated God's right of integrity by modifying God's original commandment. In other words, Adam altered God's message and meaning by his modification of God's words and his failure to attribute the source of the alteration.

Although that moral lesson is taught in the Book of Genesis, all relevant works of Jewish law on the prohibition of stealing an author's work by violating the attribution and integrity interests cite a statement from *Pirkei Avot* (*Ethics of the Fathers*), as their legal source. The importance of having one's words properly attributed to the original source is emphasized in the following verse: "Whoever repeats a thing in the name of the one who said it brings redemption to the world."[15] The commentary to this verse emphasizes that "one must display indebtedness to a source and mention him by name," essentially prohibiting taking false credit for someone else's teaching.[16] This verse also hints at the responsibility to quote a source accurately.

Ethics of the Fathers dates to the time of the *Mishnah* and its teaching about quoting sources accurately finds expression in how the Talmud itself attributes sayings to various sages. In its entirety, the Talmud underscores the importance of attribution by establishing attribution through several generations of students and teachers. For example, as used in the Talmud, the phrase "Rabbi X said" does not necessarily mean "Rabbi X himself said," but rather "Rabbi X's later disciples said in his name." As a result, authorship of the material in the Talmud cannot be equated to authorship according to our contemporary standards.[17] According to Talmudic culture, the "sayer" of a saying was understood to be repeating the traditions of his teacher and that of earlier masters. Lack of attribution is only considered wrong in cases when the original author of a saying is not obvious or known to all. In short, with respect to attribution issues, the entirety of the Talmud must be seen as the product of a flexible, collective authorship, with only *deception* constituting a breach of the duty to attribute.[18]

Interestingly, the Talmud's collaborative authorship foreshadows our current digital reality. Today, digitally created works can present great challenges for ascertaining one specific author and that author's attribution and integrity interests. In the digital era, artistic creation is often interactive and dependent upon a multitude of voices. Works are often created as a result of audience participation and reinterpretation. In this context, determining violations of an author's meaning and message is especially difficult. As our secular laws continue to evolve in response to a changing environment, I have no doubt that Jewish tradition will continue to serve as an important source of wisdom for both Jews and non-Jews.

NOTES

1 Portions of this essay are based on various sections of Roberta Rosenthal Kwall, *The Soul of Creativity: Forging a Moral Rights Law for the United States* (Stanford, CA: Stanford University Press, 2010).
2 The main character, played by Al Pacino, is actually Satan appearing on earth in the guise of a corporate lawyer.
3 See Kwall, *Soul of Creativity*, 7–8.
4 See Neil Weinstock Netanel, *From Maimonides to Microsoft: The Jewish Law of Copyright Since the Birth of Print* (New York: Oxford University Press, 2016).
5 See Kwall, *Soul of Creativity*, for a deeper exploration of the reasons for the lack of comparative protection for moral rights in the United States.
6 See Kwall, *Soul of Creativity*, 13.
7 See Daniel J. Boorstin, *The Creators: A History of Heroes of the Imagination* (New York: Vintage Books, 1992), 41.
8 Abraham R. Besdin, *Reflections of the Rav*, rev. ed. (New York: Ktav, 1993), 27–28 (quoting a lecture by Rabbi Joseph Soloveitchik).

9   See Kwall, *Soul of Creativity*, 13.

10   Rabbi Karyn D. Kedar, "The Many Names of God," in *The Women's Torah Commentary*, ed. Rabbi Elyse Goldstein (Woodstock, VT: Jewish Lights, 2000), 127, 129.

11   Kwall, *Soul of Creativity*, 14.

12   Kwall, *Soul of Creativity*, 14.

13   *B'reishit Rabbah* 19:3.

14   *Avot D'Rabbi Natan* 1:5.

15   For further discussion of this teaching, see *Pirkei Avos: Ethics of the Fathers* (New York: Mesorah, 1984), chap. 6, § 6, 59. See also Berel Wein, *Pirkei Avos: Teachings for Our Times* (New York: Shaar Press, 2003) (noting that chapter 6 is a later addition to the rest of the text, dating back to around the fourth or fifth century rather than around 200 CE).

16   Ibid.

17   Sacha Stern, "Attribution and Authorship in the Babylonian Talmud," *Journal of Jewish Studies* 45 (1994): 28, 47–48, 51.

18   Stern, "Attribution and Authorship," 51.

"You Shall Not Steal"— Ethics of Consumption

RABBI RACHEL KAHN-TROSTER

THE EIGHTH COMMANDMENT, "You shall not steal," seems straightforward and easy to fulfill. *Keep your hands off that which does not belong to you, and all will be right between you and other human beings, and between you and God.*

However, that simplicity immediately invites questions. The second half of the Ten Commandments forms a basic ethical code for a moral society. The Rabbis of the Talmud, however, expanded on this basic code and read "You shall not steal" as a reference to kidnapping—the theft of a human person.[1] This reading puts the law in the same category as the two prohibitions that precede it—those against murder and adultery, which, according to the Torah, are capital offences, while mere theft would simply require restitution and payment of fines.

While I do think that the Rabbinic inclusion of kidnapping is quite a stretch, I am intrigued by the significance of the question: what is it about theft that it can radically undermine the trust and responsibility toward others that allow for a cohesive society? Surely, the eighth commandment ("You shall not steal") implies a general ethics of justice, explicated in other parts of the Torah: You shall do right by the other members of your community. "You shall not defraud your fellow. You shall not commit robbery. The wages of a laborer shall not remain with you until morning" (Leviticus 19:13). But what is it about the general flow of money that makes it as crucial and potentially as harmful as murder?

Asking this question takes on renewed urgency today, when we are facing complicated moral questions in regard to seemingly simple issues like the ownership of goods or our relationship to the people involved in the means of their production. Already when we scratch on the mere surface of the supply chains of most of the products we buy every day—products that we may rightfully call our own—we often discover that they have been produced in ways that are fundamentally unethical. We may not ourselves steal—and yet, we are complicit in an economic system that encourages theft in various ways.

We have to admit that other human beings are exploited for our comfort and sustenance. I wish it was possible to go to the grocery store and not think about child labor in chocolate or slavery in tomatoes. I wish it was possible to buy clothes and not think about the horrific safety violations in the factories in which they are produced. I wish it was possible to perceive our purchases as simple decisions of taste budget . . . and yet, I know it is not possible.

This is a deeply uncomfortable conversation to have. However, we have to acknowledge our complicity in the misery of other human beings—by means of our consumption choices. In my work as a justice advocate, I have seen time and time again that people would rather talk about just about any other problem in the supply chain (about valid issues such as the treatment of animals, food waste, or environmental concerns, for example) than talk about how the human beings involved in food production are paid or treated.

One of my favorite midrashim is a complicated and somewhat troubling parable about theft. Commenting on the verse in Proverbs that reads, "One who shares with a thief is their own enemy; they hear the curse and do not tell" (29:24), the midrash tells the following story:

> There was a governor who used to put to death people who received stolen property, but he let the thieves go. People were angry with him, saying that he was not acting correctly. What did the governor do to convince his subjects? He issued a proclamation throughout the province, saying, "Have all the people

join me in the public field!" What did he do when they got there? He brought some weasels into the field and placed in front of them pieces of food. The weasels took the food and carried them back to their underground holes where they lived. The next day, the governor again issued a proclamation, saying, "Have all the people join me in the public field!" Again, he brought weasels and put pieces of food before them, but this time, he stopped up all the underground holes. The weasels took the food and carried them to their homes, but upon finding these stopped up, they brought their portions of food back to where they found them. The governor did this to demonstrate that all the trouble is due to the people who receive stolen property.[2]

I used to think that this midrash was harsh and that the governor vastly overreacted. Yes, it's true that there would be less oppression if we, as consumers, demanded fully transparent and fair supply chains, but that does not make us responsible—or does it? Can I say a *b'rachah* ("blessing") when I eat something that was unethically produced? If I know that a child slave laborer picked the cocoa in my chocolate, can I really celebrate Chanukah with that *gelt*? What about Passover—can I really celebrate the Jewish journey from slavery to freedom by making chocolate-covered matzah with conventional chocolate?

In the Mishnah, the Rabbis address the question of whether one can make the blessing for shaking the *lulav* over a *lulav* that is stolen or say a *b'rachah* over matzah made with stolen wheat.[3] They conclude that you cannot, and while not every act of consumption implies the fulfillment of a mitzvah, their ruling may well serve as a kind of guide for consumption generally. If we strive to live a life of holiness, then we cannot base it on the misery of others. Maimonides's commentary on the Mishnah backs up this assertion. He writes:

A mitzvah that is done by committing a transgression is not a mitzvah. Therefore, a stolen *lulav*, or one that comes from an *asheirah* [a tree used for idolatry] or a city condemned for idolatry, is invalid [for use].

Maimonides also seemingly understood our modern-day paraly-sis in the grocery store or buying clothing, however. What are we sup-posed to do when everything is produced unethically? In the *Mishneh Torah*, he discusses the problem of buying goods from a known thief:

> One may not buy stolen goods from a thief; to do so is a great transgression because it strengthens the hands of those who vi-olate the law and causes the thief to continue to steal, for if the thief would find no buyer he would not steal. . . . A thief sells his stolen wares, which the owners had not despaired of recovering; subsequently, the thief is identified and witnesses testified that the object at trial is what the thief stole. The object returns to its original owners, and the owners give to the buyer the money that was paid to the thief—due to "the enactment of the mar-ket" [*takanat hashuk*]. The owners then sue the thief to recover the money that they had to pay to the buyer. If, however, he was a known thief, the Rabbis did not apply the enactment of the market, and the owners give nothing to the buyer; rather, the buyer must sue the thief and extract from the thief the money that the buyer paid.[4]

Like the governor in our midrash, Maimonides understood that when one buys from a known thief, even if we ourselves did not steal, we create a market for stolen goods. Normally, according to Jewish law, if one unknowingly buys stolen goods, the goods are restored to their original owners, who have to sue the thief to recover their lost money. What is central for Maimonides is the concept of *takanat hashuk*—the idea that we generally buy things in good faith that they are not stolen and that we cannot be held responsible in case they are stolen. If we had to investigate the origins of everything we bought—if we truly had to worry that every single item we purchase might be stolen—the market place would collapse. No one would buy any-thing. Therefore, and according to *takanat hashuk*, we generally pun-ish the thief and hold the original owner responsible for suing the thief; however, in cases when we have to assume that we are buying stolen goods (and *takanat hashuk* is not a given anymore), we—the consumers—are held responsible, and the ones who will need to sue the thief.

So how, then, should we live in the modern economy? It seems clear that the Rabbis issued a prohibition against buying goods that we know were produced unethically. Today, we might well need to have that suspicion about everything. There are some goods, though, that are obviously of doubtful ethical standing, and each of us has to make conscious decisions about whether we are willing to buy them. There is no blanket solution. However, it seems to me that we must try to (a) avoid products whose supply chains include documented human rights abuses by (b) buying alternative products, even if that means paying a higher price, and (c) support the worker groups who are organizing to bring meaningful change to supply chains.

It is this final piece that has transformed me from merely an ethical consumer, feeling a little bit better about not directly supporting the theft of wages and other human rights abuses, into an activist. Through my work as a human rights activist at T'ruah, I have become a supporter of the Coalition of Immokalee Workers (CIW) and the Fair Food Program, a worker-designed and worker-led human rights program that has turned the Florida tomato industry from what one federal prosecutor called "ground zero for human trafficking in America" to what was hailed in the *New York Times* as the best workplace in American agriculture. The CIW—made up of workers largely from Mexico, Haiti, and Guatemala—organized together with consumer allies (including university students and people of faith, including many in the Jewish community and T'ruah's #tomatorabbis) to hold the major corporations at the top of the supply chain responsible for the sub-poverty wages and human rights abuses at the bottom. This is a novel approach: it holds the enormous grocery store chains and fast-food restaurants responsible—because of their demand for lower and lower prices for the tomatoes they purchase, as they pursue higher and higher profits—for farmworker poverty and for human rights abuses like wage theft, violence, sexual harassment, and even human trafficking. The CIW and their allies have succeeded convincing fourteen major food retailers to be part of the

Fair Food Program: the corporations agreed to pay approximately one penny more per pound of tomatoes (which goes through the supply chain straight to the paychecks of workers) and to only purchase from growers who have agreed to implement an extremely stringent human rights code, designed by the farmworkers themselves.

Since 2011, when the majority of Florida tomato growers joined the Fair Food Program, human rights for farmworkers have been overseen by the Fair Food Standards Council. These human rights, which have independent monitoring and are legally binding (two features that most corporate social responsibility programs usually sorely lack), include the right to report abuses without fear of retaliation and zero tolerance policies for wage theft, violence, and sexual harassment. A highlight of the program is worker-to-worker education: every worker on every farm is educated by a peer on their rights under the Fair Food Program, essentially turning each one of them into monitors to ensure that their rights are enforced.

Being part of the CIW's fight for justice for farmworkers also helped me realize how I could turn eating tomatoes into a holy act. I was tired of being told I could be a more ethical consumer by buying a better product. It was a focus on things, not on people. After all, it is not the tomato but the tomato worker who is created in the image of God. As Jewish activists, we are driven by the Torah's mandate to pursue justice by upholding the rights of and standing in solidarity with the workers. Fighting for food justice means ensuring the human rights and wages of agricultural workers, and doing so places the needs, dignity, and expertise of the workers at the head of the table.

I shook myself out of my paralysis over not being able to make every purchase an ethical one and channeled my energy into being part of a moment for sector-wide change. Thanks to Fair Food Program, tens of thousands of tomato workers—not just in Florida but now along the entire East Coast—make higher wages and have guaranteed human rights in the field. The CIW's model of worker-led and worker-designed human rights in supply chains (called worker-driven social responsibility) has expanded to global garment workers, Vermont dairy workers, and construction workers in the Midwest and hopefully soon to many more locations and industries. Yes, I feel good when I buy tomatoes with a Fair Food label, but not just because I know I was not purchasing unethically. It is because in an effort to avoid violating "You shall not steal," I participated in the mitzvah of *tikkun olam*.

NOTES

1 *Babylonian Talmud, Sanhedrin* 86a.
2 *Vayikra Rabbah* 6:2.
3 *Mishnah Sukkah* 3:1.
4 Maimonides, *Mishneh Torah, Hilchot G'neivah* 5:1.

Ninth Commandment

לֹא-תַעֲנֶה בְרֵעֲךָ עֵד שָׁקֶר:

You shall not bear false witness against your neighbor.
—Exodus 20:13

Don't Be That Person

RABBI MICHAEL MARMUR, PhD

THE NINTH COMMANDMENT ought to be easy to understand. Five short Hebrew words express a direct interdiction: *one should not bear false testimony regarding one's fellow human being.*

Philo and Ibn Ezra

My attempt here is to understand what this commandment might mean for us as we encounter it in a Western twenty-first-century setting. In support of this goal, it is helpful to refer to some eminent readers of the Decalogue from history, particularly Philo of Alexandria (Egypt, first century CE) and Abraham ibn Ezra (1089–1167). Taken together, these commentators, two of the finest minds the Jewish people have known, offer a premodern basis for a contemporary reading of this commandment, one that raises fundamental questions.

Infused by a commitment to the ways of the Jews as he knew them and immersed in the Hellenistic philosophy and aesthetic of his day, Philo of Alexandria offered a number of explanations of the commandment. He starts with the assertion that those who bear false witness are guilty of corrupting truth, "a treasure as sacred as anything we possess in life, which like the sun pours lights on facts and events."[1] He makes use here of the Greek word *aletheia*, truth in the sense of uncovering, revealing, shedding light in dark corners. It is the opposite of *lethe*, which stands for oblivion, forgetfulness, or concealment. To speak falsely as a witness is to cast a shadow where there should be light. It is an offense against truth.

Ibn Ezra rarely confessed to being perplexed by a word or phrase. However, when confronted with the ninth commandment, he was struck by a linguistic anomaly: "I have spent many years searching for the reason that the text reads *eid shaker*, 'a false witness,' and not *eidut shaker*, 'false testimony.'" Ibn Ezra is grappling with a phrase that ought to refer to testimony in general, but instead refers to a particular individual.

David Kimchi, who was born shortly before Ibn Ezra died, solved this problem by positing that *eid* is a word that can be deployed both in its specific sense—"a witness"—and also in an abstracted sense—"witness," "testimony." Commenting on this question in the nineteenth century, Samuel David Luzzatto suggested that an extra noun is presumed, though absent, and that the verse should be read to mean: "Do not give the testimony of a false witness." For Kimchi and Luzzatto then, the problem haunting Ibn Ezra was simply an issue of idiom.

Ibn Ezra, however, offered a more radical and daring reading of the commandment. It should be read as an exhortation directed at the false witness: "You, O false witness, do not offer testimony. If you are a false witness, do not testify at all." He concludes by suggesting that the spirit of the commandment is that of the words to be found in the Holiness Code, Leviticus 19:11: "You shall not deal deceitfully or falsely with one another."[2]

What the Commandment Doesn't Say

It is striking that the Decalogue does *not* include a normative insistence on telling the truth or avoiding its opposite. One might have imagined that a version of "Thou shalt tell the truth" or "Thou shalt not lie" would have found its way in, but it did not.

Such adjurations are known in the Hebrew Bible. The prophet Zechariah reports these as the words of God:

> Execute true judgment, and let every person show mercy and compassion to their kin. (Zechariah 7:9)

> These are the things you shall do: speak you the truth every

person with their fellow, execute the judgment of truth and peace in your gates. And let none of you design evil in your heart against your neighbor, and love no false oath. (Zechariah 8:16–17)

Love truth and peace. (Zechariah 8:19)

The Book of Exodus itself includes a stirring moral pronouncement: "Keep far from a false charge; do not bring death on those who are innocent and in the right" (Exodus 23:7).

Instead of such a general prohibition, however, the Exodus and Deuteronomy versions of the Decalogue offer two variations on the same specific theme, limited to the question of testimony as described at greater length in Exodus 23 and most particularly in Deuteronomy 19, where the fate of the deceiver is established: that which the false witness would have done to the innocent party is to be done to the deceiver.

Historical and Contemporary Problems with Truth

Truth has always been a rare commodity. A Talmudic teaching points out that the word *emet*, "truth," comprises the first, middle, and last letters of the Hebrew alphabet; they could not be farther apart. The word *sheker*, "lie," is comprised of letters adjacent to each other. Based on these observations, the Talmud concludes that "a lie is common, while the truth is rare."[3]

Truth is also highly contested in our own age. Its meaning and very existence are debated within and between philosophical schools. Theories of truth abound; a recent authoritative work lists five classic approaches, which range from correspondence through coherence, pragmatism, deflationism, and semantic theories.[4] Absolutists, skeptics, and relativists propound fundamentally different hypotheses on this and most other questions and often talk past each other: "The absolutist trumpets his plain vision; the relativist sees only someone who is unaware of his own spectacles."[5]

To live in the twenty-first century is to encounter problems with the meaning of truth to a degree perhaps unprecedented in history. This is due not solely to the preponderance of contradictory understandings of the term, but also to cultural and technological changes that make it harder than ever to know what can be considered true. On the one hand, to use Philo's metaphor, there has never been as much access to "the light of truth," since data is accessible and millions can be, in a sense, present at events that in previous generations would have been attended by hundreds. On the other hand, however, it has never been so easy for interested parties to divert and corrupt the light we regard as the light of truth in pursuit of their own commercial or political agendas.

The plurality of our options and the unreliability of our perceptions make the pursuit of truth a perplexing and often paralyzing undertaking. In a 2018 symposium on truth and "truthiness" held by Hebrew Union College–Jewish Institute of Religion, Dahlia Lithwick predicted that within a few months or years there will be technology widely available that will make it extremely hard to tell if the evidence of our own eyes is to be trusted; we will see footage of someone saying something, but we won't be able to tell if this is an accurate reflection of what has taken place or a fake, a fabricated concoction designed to confuse or misinform. Dazzled by manufactured light, it is hard to recognize the truth when we see it.

Felipe Fernández-Armesto offers distinctions between four kinds of truth. First he lists "the truth you feel," then "the truth you are told." The third phase he calls both "the truth of reason" and "the truth you think for yourself," and the list is completed by "the truth you perceive through your senses."[6] For most of us most of the time, our experience of the truth is impacted by all of these strata simultaneously—we intuit truth, take it on trust, deduce it, and perceive it. However, in a postmodern age, many question or deny its very existence (although that skepticism is often selective)!

Postmodern critics of old-fashioned truth discourse have challenged some of our most persistent assumptions. Michel Foucault once made this point in an interview, in a characteristically provocative way: "I think that, instead of trying to find out what truth, as opposed to error, is, it might be more interesting to take up the problem posed by Nietzsche: how is it that, in our societies, 'the truth' has been given this value, thus placing us absolutely under its thrall?"[7] Foucault, whose emphasis tended to be on relations of power within social structures, was keen to decentralize this abstract notion of "truth" and to recognize that often the One Great Truth that we hold to be Out There is an expression of an agenda.

Richard Rorty offers a distinction between two schools, roughly equivalent to pre-moderns and modernists in one corner and post-modernists in the opposite corner. He calls them metaphysicians and ironists. It is the former who insist "that what matters is not what language is being used but what is *true*."[8] The ironist, on the other hand, holds that sentences such as "'is independent of the human mind' are simply platitudes used to inculcate . . . the common sense of the West." When an ironist reflects on this search for a better vocabulary, the description "is dominated by metaphors of making rather than finding, of diversification and novelty rather than con-vergence to the antecedently present."[9]

It would appear that the gulf separating these approaches is unbridgeable, that metaphysicians and ironists, absolutists and rel-ativists, modernists and postmodernists, may not agree on anything regarding the truth, since the most fundamental questions of what that might mean are radically contested. When ironists invoke Fried-rich Nietzsche and Michel Foucault saying that there are no facts, only interpretations, they see in these provocative words a strident and necessary corrective to a kind of naïve credulity. Others, how-ever, see such views as dangerously close not only to a shapeless relativism, but also to a self-serving self-justification with alarming moral implications.

Karl Lueger was the mayor of Vienna until his death in 1910. A man of many contradictions, he seemed to espouse antisemitic views while maintaining close personal relations with a number of people of Jewish descent. Challenged to defend this apparent hypoc-risy, Lueger is said to have responded, "*I decide who is a Jew*." His remark was to become one of the dark slogans of the twentieth cen-tury, emblematic of the risk and tragedy implicit in the loss of faith in a Great Truth Out There. In its absence, the truth may be colonized by the strong, the unscrupulous, and the perverse. Contemporary history serves as a reminder of what is at stake in this debate about the nature of truth. The metaphysicians hold that once the notion of a truth external to my perception has gone, the potential for double-speak and deception is increased. The ironists respond that hanging on to an indefensible concept of truth "out there" is itself an instrument of domination and manipulation. What to do?

Truth and Testimony

Most of what we take to be true we take on trust. The testimony of a star witness or the weather forecaster, a starred academic or a seasoned veteran, our website of choice or our favored political leader—this often provides the basis of what we believe to be true. Philosophers have tended to focus on what we can assert to be true based on something other than hearsay or doctrine. Many of them turn our senses, our instincts, and our impressions into witnesses to be cross-examined by our reason to judge if their testimony is to be accepted. Whether we are judging the credibility of an external expert or testing our own assumptions, we are attempting to arrive at truth through the consideration of testimony. Spinoza expressed this with characteristic brilliance:

> The original sense of *true* and *false* seems to have arisen with narratives. A story was called true when it told of events that had actually befallen, and false when it told of events that had not occurred at all. But philosophers later took over this notion to signify the fit of an idea with its object, or vice versa. So an idea is called true when it presents itself as it really is, and false when it presents itself otherwise. For ideas are nothing but stories, mental histories of nature. But this notion in turn was shifted, to apply metaphorically to mute things, as when we call gold true or false, as if what is presented to us as gold were telling its own story about what it is or is not in itself.[10]

Spinoza argues that even for strict adherents to the correspondence theory of truth (namely, that a statement is true to the degree that it can be shown to correspond to facts in the natural world), there is

still a story being told. In each case, we are asked to judge whether the
account—which may be given by live individuals, by ancient texts,
or by inanimate objects—is plausible. Even when I sit in solitude
and ponder an abstract idea, I am in some sense cross-examining a
witness.

Testimony is not only an abstract concern of philosophy. It has
become one of the most pressing cultural and political issues of our
time.[11] The question is often posed from the perspective of the individual, struggling to make sense of a dizzying array of truth claims.
The ninth commandment relates to the issue from the point of view
of the person called upon to offer testimony. It does not offer a guide
to the consumer of potential truths, but rather sets down guidelines
for their purveyors. It asks each one of us whether we plan to contribute to the flood of disinformation in the world or to speak, as much
as we can, words of truth.

Looking Again at the Commandment: Three Central Terms

I read the ninth commandment against the backdrop of these contemporary debates. It is remarkable for its limited scope, its specific-
ity. It sets aside the abstractions of truth and focuses instead on the
way I should act when bringing testimony. The original context of
this commandment was juridical: when bearing witness in relation
to one's fellow person (the word employed, *rei-ah*, implies a degree of
affinity with this person), one may not be a lying witness.[12]

Taaneh and *Sheker*

The term employed for bearing witness here and elsewhere in the
Hebrew Bible[13] is a particular idiomatic form of a verb whose basic
meaning is "to answer, to respond." This usage implies testimony
to the detriment of the defendant. When bearing a witness in a way
that may harm your fellow human being, you may not act as "___"
and here the two versions differ in their terminology. The medieval
exegete Don Isaac Abarbanel suggests that the term employed in
Deuteronomy, *shav*, has a wider meaning than *sheker* in the Exodus
version. *Sheker* means "a lie, a falsehood," while *shav* (often translated

as "vanity") covers lies as well as *kazav* ("something that misleads or disappoints") and *batalah* ("nullity," "something of little worth," "a waste"). In the Deuteronomy version, it is not just the utterance of a lie that is forbidden, but rather anything irrelevant, nihilistic, wasteful, or confusing.

A statement can be accurate but misleading. My father recalls a teacher of his telling the tale of a captain of a ship constantly at loggerheads with the vessel's first mate. Each day both men had to write a report in the log. One day the captain wrote, "Today, the first mate was drunk." In order to exact his revenge, the following day the first mate wrote, "Today, the captain was *not* drunk." It is possible that neither of these statements was a lie, a *sheker*. But at least one of them falls clearly into the category of *shav*.

Accuracy and truth are not the same thing. I may speak the truth to the best of my ability and still my testimony may be mistaken.[14] Or like the first mate, I may avoid telling an outright lie, but my intentions may be false. The ninth commandment calls each of us to account in the way we relate to our fellow person, in court and outside it. As in Ibn Ezra's dialogic reading, it speaks to each of us at the very moment when we are poised to deceive, and it says to us: Don't be that person. Don't add to the bulging ocean of falsity in the world. It implies that we would be better served diverting our thoughts and our words to an endangered reservoir, in which words offered in sincerity and true testimonies are stored.

The ninth commandment is addressed to the ironist and to the metaphysician, to those who believe that there is no Great Overarching Truth and to those who believe in that Truth with all their heart. To both this commandment speaks, whether it is heard in Philo's abstractions or Ibn Ezra's concrete conversation.

REI-ECHA

This word *rei-ah* to denote your fellow human is the same word found in Leviticus 19:18, where we are commanded to love this *rei-ah* even as we love ourselves. As I read the ninth commandment, this parallel between the other and oneself also stands. Just as we are enjoined to avoid falsity and deception with the other, we are also being told a version of the words Shakespeare placed in the mouth of Polonius:

> To thine own self be true
> And it must follow as night the day,
> Thou canst not be false to any man.[15]

There is an assumption at the heart of this commandment. The assumption is that when we speak in regard to our fellow human being, we have a sense of when we are speaking in truth and when we lie. I am enough of an ironist to believe that we often lack vigilance in our defense of the truth. We fool ourselves and are incentivized by many around us to avoid searching for the truth. This is true in the supermarket, and the synagogue, and the senate house. It relates to what we tell ourselves about the health of our planet and the stability of our political systems, just as it relates to what we tell ourselves about our calorific intake and our ethical output. But there is such a thing as integrity no less for ironists than for metaphysicians. A scoundrel is a scoundrel, whichever prophet they hide behind.

The insistent voice of these five words beseeches us personally: When you respond to the other, you are facing yourself. Don't lie or spout spurious irrelevances. Don't deceive or intone vanities. Don't obfuscate. Don't throw the other guy under the bus and don't edit so as to place yourself in a good light. Don't obscure what Philo saw as the great light of truth. Don't be that person.

We may not have a clear sense of how to navigate the challenges of truth and truthiness, post-truth and fake news. But however we are to proceed, we will have need of people who hear this biblical utterance as a personal call. If we are to make it, we shouldn't be that person, the false witness. We should be better than that.

Notes

1   Philo, *De Decalogo*, 138.
2   For more on the relationship between the Decalogue and the Holiness Code, see Julian Morgenstern, "The Decalogue of the Holiness Code," *Hebrew Union College Annual* 26 (1955): 1–27.

3   *Babylonian Talmud, Shabbat* 104a.

4   Simon Blackburn, *On Truth* (New York: Oxford University Press, 2018). For another vigorous presentation of different understandings of truth, see Lenn E. Goodman, *In Defence of Truth: A Pluralistic Approach* (New York: Humanity Books, 2001).

5   Simon Blackburn, *Truth: A Guide for the Perplexed* (London: Penguin, 2006), xix.

6   Felipe Fernández-Armesto, *Truth: A History and a Guide for the Perplexed* (London: Black Swan, 1998).

7   Walter Truett Anderson, ed., *The Truth about the Truth: De-confusing and Re-constructing the Postmodern World* (New York: Putnam's, 1995), 45.

8   Anderson, 102.

9   Anderson, 104.

10 Spinoza, *Cogitata Metaphysica* VI, quoted and discussed in Goodman, *In Defence of Truth*, 383f.

11 For a discussion of testimony as a problem in philosophy, see C. A. J. Coady, *Testimony: A Philosophical Study* (Oxford: Clarendon, 1992). For some resonances of this theme in wider contexts, see Bob Plant, "On Testimony, Sincerity and Truth," *Paragraph* 30, no. 1 (2007): 30–50; and Nora Strejilevich, "Testimony: Beyond the Language of Truth," *Human Rights Quarterly* 6, no. 3 (2006): 701–13.

12 For a discussion of the development of this theme in later Jewish law, see Shamma Friedman, "The 'Plotting Witness' and Beyond: A Continuum in Ancient Near Eastern, Biblical and Talmudic Law," in *Birkat Shalom: Studies in the Bible, Ancient Near Eastern Literature, and Postbiblical Judaism*, vol. 2, ed. Chaim Cohen et al. (Winona Lake: Eisenbrauns, 2008), 801–29.

13 See Genesis 30:33; Numbers 35:30; Deuteronomy 19:16, 19:18; I Samuel 12:3; II Samuel 1:16; Isaiah 3:9, 59:12; Jeremiah 14:7; Micah 6:3; Proverbs 25:18; Job 15:6, 16:8; Ruth 1:21.

14 New scientific research is teaching much about how inaccurate testimony may be given without malice. See, for example, Jeffrey W. Sherman, Carla J. Groom, Katja Ehrenberg, and Karl Christoph Klauer, "Bearing False Witness under Pressure: Implicit and Explicit Components of Stereotype-Driven Memory Distortions," *Social Cognition* 21, no. 3 (2003): 213–46.

15 *Hamlet*, act 1, scene 3. In their original context these words may have an ironic or self-seeking connotation.

"Fake News" and Its Challenges to Journalism

BATYA UNGAR-SARGON, PhD

I GREW UP in the golden age of optical illusions.

There were those "seeing-eye" images, framed in basement play-rooms and dentists' offices where, if you squinted hard enough, a 3-D image would come to life inside of what had just moments earlier been a flat pattern. I remember standing for hours in front of those pictures and the excruciating effort it took to relax my eyes to just the right degree until the promised scene—"Attacking Lion" or "Lake Como"—suddenly appeared.

There were also easier ones that you found on cards and later in psychology textbooks. There was the one that was a rabbit if you looked at it this way and a duck if you looked at it that way. Another one was a beautiful woman in a mink stole, who morphed into an old woman with a wart on her nose and a look of resignation on her face, if you looked at it from another angle. I loved those optical illusions, loved toggling back and forth between the duck and the rabbit, the old and young women, the vase and the two faces. I found them hyp-notizing: What did it *mean* that I could see two versions of the same image? That I could by turns be a duck-seer and a rabbit-seer? What part of me could inhabit both sides of this visual pun by turns, but never both at once?

These images came to signify for me the value of ambiguity and the importance of a nimble, empathic mind that is able to see the two sides of a thing—that is able to *enjoy* seeing the two sides of a thing! No doubt, there were duck people and rabbit people; left to their own devices my own eyes were inarguably biased in the duck's favor. But almost everyone could toggle, especially once you pointed out the rabbit's nose.

It was a simpler time.

Today, the art of the toggle has all but disappeared.

Instead of staring at rabbit-ducks, we stare at a dress that half the world sees as blue and half sees as gold, but no one can see as both. Instead of being intrigued by a woman by turns old and young, we are divided over an audio clip that half the world hears as "yanny" and half as "laurel." Not one person comes forward who claims to hear both.

It's not only the art of the toggle that's been lost. It's the *value* of the toggle, too. Instead of poring over images and explaining how to see things differently, we discuss the smirking Catholic schoolboys who mobbed a Native American elder—or who were accosted by him, depending on who you are. We watch a man making his way to the Supreme Court despite sexually assaulting a young girl when he was a teenager—or despite the mob that sought to ruin his life.

It is of no value to anyone at all to convince those on the other side to see things as they do. We have become a nation of people unable to see things as the other half does and unable to comprehend how any decent person could disagree with us. We only speak to people we agree with. We only read people we agree with, only read articles written by and for people with our values.

Our testimony is only for those who see blue, those who hear "laurel." Or those who see gold and hear "yanny." The age of rabbit seers lovingly tracing the rabbit's nose as a member of the duck crowd gasps with surprise is no more. Our nation of togglers has become a nation blinkered. We will do anything to avoid having to see things as the other half does.

The Torah gave us many reasons to be proud. One of them is its focus on criminal justice. The liberal American Jewish value of Jewish social justice work—which sees making the world into a more just place as the primary mandate of our tradition—is deeply embedded in our sacred texts: Genesis 18:19, Exodus 23:9, Deuteronomy

15:7–8, Deuteronomy 16:20, Isaiah 1:17, Jeremiah 9:23, Hosea 10:12, Proverbs 10:2, and so on.

The focus on criminal justice is present in every aspect of Jewish law dealing with state power—from the requirement of having two witnesses, to the required warning before someone can be considered liable for their sins, to the repeated mandate that judges be impartial and never prioritize the rich or the poor. And of course, there is the commandment to us all to chase after justice at all costs.

Our tradition has commanded us to fight for these values, values that are especially important in this day and age. This is a time of rampant injustice against minorities in the American criminal justice system. These injustices include the mass incarceration of African American males, unconstitutional stop and frisk policies and other broken-window policing that effectively criminalizes the poor, racial bias in the judicial system, the horrifically unjust cash bail system, and other ways in which this country has failed to ensure all its citizens due process.

One of the Ten Commandments is the prohibition against false testimony: *lo taaneh v'rei-acha eid shaker*, which translates as "You shall not respond to your friend as a lying witness."[1] This commandment, the ninth, has been interpreted in the context of a court of law. Given what we know about the unreliability of witness testimony, this commandment has never been more important than today. Black and brown people especially have fallen victim to the biases of court witnesses.

However, the wording of the biblical commandment makes it applicable to a much broader context: "You shall not respond—*taaneh*—to your friend as a lying witness." My great-great-great-great-grandfather, the Netziv, wrote in his commentary on the Torah, the *Ha'ameik Davar*, that the reason the Torah uses the word *taaneh*, "you shall not *respond*," is because the prohibition is not just against testifying falsely, which is included in the prohibition against lying. Bringing your expertise to bear on a situation in a way that is false or that encourages others to come to a false conclusion is its own sin–but it is worse to testify against a friend. Why is that?

A few chapters later, the Torah returns to the word *taaneh* to explore further what this prohibition against giving false testimony means:

> You shall not be the bearer of a frivolous report; join not your hand with an evil person to be a witness of violent corruption. Don't be following a crowd to do wrong; neither shall you *respond* to a fight by following the crowd to pervert the outcome. Don't even prefer a poor man in his fight. And when you meet your enemy's ox or donkey walking astray, you must—you *must*—return it to him." (Exodus 23:1–4)[2]

These laws make it clear that the prohibition against giving false testimony is part of a series of laws commanding the Jewish people not only to be honest both inside and outside of the courtroom, but also to be impartial actors. This is hardest to do when testifying for or against a friend.

According to the Torah, group pressure is inherently corrupting. To counterbalance that pressure, the Torah commands us to make up our own minds, to decide for ourselves. Following the crowd *is* wrong, for a crowd is in and of itself a form of violent power, says the Torah. Individualism and individual responsibility get lost in crowds, which makes them fundamentally violent and fundamentally incapable of securing justice. The Torah tells us not to follow a crowd to do wrong and, right after, not even to prefer a poor person in a dispute. God commands us to resist the pressure applied by others, even when they share our own values. It is only by resisting the crowd that a Jew can do the right thing. It is only by resisting the crowd that one can *choose* to do the right thing.

Just as group pressure should not prevent us from choosing justice, the Torah goes on, so too our own personal histories are no justification for failing to do the right thing. Thus, even our enemies' property deserves our goodwill. The Torah, always sensitive to human nature, knows that even a good Jew will struggle to help an enemy's lost donkey find its way home.

Even more moving is the Torah's assumption that it is addressing social justice warriors. It tells us as its readers not to favor the poor over the rich. However, it does not even consider it necessary to warn us not to do the opposite: to favor the rich over the poor (that comes much later, in the Book of Deuteronomy)! In other words, the Torah believes that Jews are naturally inclined to favor the poor over the rich. And it is this natural—and inherently empathetic—inclination that we must resist, too.

What all these commandments insist upon is that we have to choose for ourselves the just path and not allow our personal histories, group pressure, or our own values to decide for us.

It is that value of independent thought that the Torah holds up as an inherent component to justice.

We live in incredibly divided times. Our current leader is a man who is the embodiment of the most cartoonish qualities of the "yannys." Not only that, but he has realized that the key to power is attention and that the key to getting attention is to heighten the differences between the "laurels" and the "yannys" to an absurd degree. In order to protect ourselves from his incessant gaslighting and to reassure ourselves of the accuracy of our own opinion, we have become a nation of people who retreat into ever-smaller tribes for comfort. Safely ensconced in Facebook algorithms that protect us from the views of others, we are emboldened in our truths, empowered by our righteousness, alleviated of our doubts. Of course, to us, our side seems to be the side of righteousness. It is the side of helping the immigrant, a value so dear to the Torah's beating heart that it's mentioned thirty-six times. Our side is the side of women's rights, assisting the poor, not tearing babies from their mothers' arms, and raising up the voices of the disenfranchised. Surely the Torah would approve of this tribe and disapprove of the other. After all, our tribe is the one following the Torah's commandments.

That may be true. But the Torah also warns against blindly following a crowd. It even warns against following our own best instincts to favor the poor in a legal dispute. Choose for yourself, the Torah says. Find a way to understand why your side might be *wrong*, and why the other side might be *right*, even if you ultimately find that you *are* right. Spend some time thinking about the arguments of the other side.

The Torah wants us to be independent thinkers. In other words, it wants us to be togglers. If you cannot see things from the perspective of the other side, you have no way of knowing whether your own argument is thorough. If you cannot understand and empathize with someone who might have arrived at a different conclusion, you can never be certain why you arrived at your conclusion: Because of the facts you gathered? Because of your emotions? Because of the crowd around you who shares them? Until you can see the rabbit, you are not *choosing* to see the duck. The image of the duck is just the image that came to you naturally, given your own inclinations. This is not who the Torah asks us to be as Jews. Instead, it asks us to constantly question whether we are right. It asks us to put aside even our strongest emotions in order to pursue justice. It asks us to have empathy for our enemies, to respect their boundaries and their way of life. This empathy *is* justice, the Torah tells us. The truth is not to be found in the pressure of a crowd, but in the loneliness of resisting the crowd, of speaking truth to the power of our own convictions.

This is a difficult, complex thought. It has never been more important than it is today.

A liberal democracy is built on tolerating the opinions of others. However, today, we spend all of our energy being outraged at a visceral level at those whose views we do not share, labeling them with ugly monikers, and demanding that no one normalize them. We believe there are thoughts that are off-limits, as are any thoughts that might be adjacent to those thoughts.

In losing the ability to understand the other side, we have lost the ability to honestly see ourselves, which carries with it an inability to adjudicate, an inability to pursue justice, and an inability to convince others to care about what we care about. We must learn again the art of the toggle and teach it to our children. Instead of demonizing the other, we must learn to think like them, even if we ultimately prefer to see the old lady instead of the young one, the vase instead of the two faces, the duck instead of the rabbit.

This isn't just a mitzvah. It is currently an issue of national security. As many have noted, the Russian interference in the 2016 election was not done with the purpose of electing President Trump; its purpose was to undermine democracy by exacerbating the divisions in American society. Thanks to these disinformation campaigns that go viral on social media, our own values, even our own emotions, have become weaponized against us, have been made into tools in a battlefield for the heart and soul of this country—its democracy. The feeling of righteous indignation is not the hallmark of justice; it is rather the sign that we are being played. We must make ourselves less fertile grounds for such attacks, both for the health of our nation and because the Torah commands it.

The ninth commandment is the commandment that requires us to give accurate testimony. Built into this commandment is the ability to see things as others do and to choose justice.

We who care about *tikkun olam*, justice, Torah values, and this great country that has given us a home must learn again the art of the toggle—before it is too late.

NOTES
1   Author's translation.
2   Author's translation.

TENTH COMMANDMENT

לֹא תַחְמֹד בֵּית רֵעֶךָ לֹא־תַחְמֹד אֵשֶׁת
רֵעֶךָ וְעַבְדֹּו וַאֲמָתֹו וְשֹׁורֹו וַחֲמֹרֹו וְכֹל
אֲשֶׁר לְרֵעֶךָ:

*You shall not covet your neighbor's house: you
shall not covet your neighbor's wife, nor male
nor female slave, nor ox nor ass, nor anything
that is your neighbor's.*

—Exodus 20:14

Torah's Thought Crime?

Rabbi Barry H. Block

When Jimmy Carter was running for president in 1976, he (in)famously told *Playboy*, "I've looked on many women with lust. I've committed adultery in my heart many times."[1] Carter's confession was controversial in its day, which is hard to believe forty-plus years later. Even in the 1970s, though, Jewish Americans' reaction might best have been characterized as "Nu?" Elaborating, a Jew might have said (and many did), "Well, of course, Governor Carter has lusted after people who aren't his wife. Virtually every married person does. The only pertinent question is whether he committed adultery," for which there was never any evidence.

Rava, sage of the Babylonian Talmud, famously proclaimed, "Matters of the heart are not matters."[2] In other words, Judaism holds that every human being possesses *yetzer hara* ("the evil inclination") but we are not guilty unless we act upon it. It is strange, then, that the tenth commandment seems to prohibit a mere desire to sin: "You shall not covet your neighbor's house: you shall not covet your neighbor's wife, nor male nor female slave, nor ox nor ass, nor anything that is your neighbor's" (Exodus 20:14). While we can well imagine the corrosive complications of craving romantic partners and material possessions prohibited to us, the desire itself hardly seems criminal.

Many have suggested that coveting is no different from the crimes to which it could lead, namely, stealing and adultery. Carter, for example, quoted Christian Scripture (Matthew 5:28) to that effect: "Christ said, 'I tell you that anyone who looks on a woman with lust has in his heart already committed adultery.'"[3] Modern Bible scholars would argue that Jesus has a point. In the *Tanach*, the roots typically translated as "covet" (*chet-mem-dalet*) and "take" (*lamed-kuf-chet*) are often utilized interchangeably.[4] Examples include Deuteronomy 7:25, "You shall not covet the silver and gold on them and keep it for yourselves"; and Joshua 7:21, "I saw among the spoil a fine Shinar mantle . . . and I coveted and took them."[5] The interconnectedness of the two verbs is most apparent in Micah 2:2, "They covet fields and seize them; Houses, and take them away."

But there's a problem. Classical Torah commentators cannot tolerate the apparent biblical redundancy that would result from the tenth commandment's being a recapitulation of the seventh and eighth, the prohibitions of adultery and theft. Therefore, thirteenth-century French Torah commentator Rabbi Hezekiah ben Manoah doesn't quite equate lust with adultery: "Since there is already a prohibition against adultery, this means you should not try to get your neighbor to divorce his wife so you can marry her."[6] For Hezekiah, the tenth commandment prohibits behavior that is not technically adultery but instead an otherwise legal act to achieve the same wicked end. Hezekiah's Catalan contemporary Nachmanides focuses on property, but otherwise makes a similar comment: "Anyone who is judged to owe something to another person . . . but does not covetously desire something that belongs to somebody else, shall simply pay what is owed."[7] Our covetous desires do not make us into sinners, as long as our actual behavior remains moral.

Two centuries earlier, the Spanish commentator Abraham ibn Ezra suggested that the tenth commandment really is a thought crime, namely a prohibition against entertaining particularly pernicious and destructive dictates of *yetzer hara*, the evil inclination that each person is understood to harbor.

But what if a person were to desire sexual intimacy with an immediate relative? By inference, Ibn Ezra suggests that incestuous or adulterous urges—and, we might add, an eagerness to steal—are the tenth commandment's targets. In short, "You shall not covet" is an injunction against *yetzer hara* itself.

How can the *Tanach* forbid an inclination with which God has created us? And supposing that we could expel *yetzer hara*, should we do so? After all, despite its name—*ra* does mean "evil"—our Rabbis do not view our *yetzer hara* as exclusively evil. Without it, they say, a human being would never marry, procreate, build a house, or earn a living.[8]

We all demonstrate moral failings that are remarkably similar to our greatest achievements. We fight our *yetzer hara* with ambivalence, seeking to conquer our bad behavior without sacrificing its benefits:

- The temptation to cheat on our taxes (to steal from the government) comes from the same impulse that drives our success at work.
- The allure of glancing over at the next student's test paper is the very same that pushes a person to do well in school.
- The urge to lie for our kids overcomes us precisely because we are so devoted to wanting the best for them.
- The stinginess that makes a person uncharitable seems inseparable from the thrift by which the same individual has provided for a secure retirement.
- The failure to express thanks for another's kindness or to make room for another's success may stem from laudable self-reliance.

We can understand why our Sages struggled with the tenth commandment's apparent attempt to outlaw *yetzer hara*, even to the point of recasting it as a prohibition against wicked action rather than thought. God has implanted a most complicated instinct within us: we must express our evil inclination in order to accomplish anything in this world, and we must restrain that very same impulse if we are not to be evil.

What, then, is a person to do, seeking to keep far from evil, the apparent purpose for the coveting prohibition?

Rabbi Stephen Fuchs offers the unlikely example of Ebenezer Scrooge, from *A Christmas Carol*, by Charles Dickens. Scrooge is as successful at business as he is miserly. The nightmares that lead to his repentance begin when he sees his late partner, Jacob Marley, as "he walks about [the afterlife] chained to his account books, wailing in misery." Scrooge objects: "But you were always a good man of business, Jacob!" And that he was. Indeed, Marley's obsession with amassing and preserving his fortune had been intimately connected to his stinginess, the principal manifestation of his evil inclination.

Ultimately, Scrooge recognizes Marley's problem as his own. By the time the story reaches its conclusion, he has found a way to turn away from the wicked results of his natural impulses without sacrificing the benefits. Scrooge can perpetuate his success at work—indeed he must, to continue employing Bob Cratchit—in order to provide for Tiny Tim, his worker's lovable and gravely ill son.[9]

The tenth commandment must not be commanding us to obliterate our *yetzer hara*, for that would be both impossible and inadvisable. Our task instead is to redirect that inclination to do only good:

- Those who must stop cheating on their taxes—a form of stealing, after all—may channel their financial wizardry into helping a charitable organization to balance its books.
- Students who sneak peeks at classmates' tests should redirect their eagerness for good grades by helping a student who has a harder time. Tutoring somebody else will sharpen one's own skills.
- Been lying for your kids? Channel that poorly spent energy into a mitzvah. A less fortunate child could use your help to get ahead in life.
- Others, as stingy as Scrooge, might keep working and earning and saving, while also utilizing their fiscal acumen to create and stick to a generous charitable budget. That may be hard work at first, but the miser is no stranger to effort. The payoff will be immeasurable.
- People who have taken self-reliance to an extreme, failing to acknowledge the gifts and contributions of others, may make it their business to build up the esteem of others, spreading gratitude around their homes, workplaces, and communities.

- For many, the most powerful of urges is sexual. The same passion that inclines a person to sexual immorality may be redirected to the people with the rightful claim upon one's love and devotion.

An eighteenth-century Polish rabbi known as the Dubner Maggid told a wonderful story to illustrate the point:

> A king owned a precious diamond, his prized possession. One morning, he awakened to find, to his horror, that the diamond had sustained a hideous scratch. How could such a thing even have happened? The king had slept with the diamond that night as every night, hugging it close. The king called upon skilled artisans throughout the land. Each of them responded identically: "I can't imagine how that happened. Nothing is harder than a diamond. And I have no idea how to remove the scratch." The king called experts from across the sea, and even consulted magicians and seers, but none could help. Finally, a young girl stepped forward. "I think I can repair the diamond," she said. The eager king entrusted her with the jewel. The next day, the girl returned the diamond. Now, the gem was emblazoned with the etching of a rose. What had been a scratch was now the stem of a magnificent flower. The king was mightily pleased.[10]

The story is allegory. The scratch stands for the wrongs we have done. They cannot be erased. Indeed, the evil impulse that gives rise to sins cannot be obliterated. However, one can, with hard work and artistry, turn even *yetzer hara* into a thing of beauty. The king represents God. The Holy One is distressed by our sins, desiring nothing more than for us to employ our wicked impulse to positive purpose. As for the diamond, that jewel is the human soul, hanging ever in the balance. The scratches are as unavoidable as *yetzer hara* itself.

Jimmy Carter was wrong, at least from a Jewish perspective. If a married person lusts after a person who is not his or her spouse, no sin has been committed. Instead, to the extent we can know anyone only from his public persona, the evidence from President Carter's life is that he has directed that passion lovingly and exclusively to his wife of more than seventy years, Rosalynn. But the thirty-ninth president of the United States—or Jesus, whom Carter quotes—is not the only one who has failed to grasp the true intent of the tenth commandment. Nachmanides and Hezekiah ben Manoah seem to protest too eagerly when they insist that "You shall not covet" means that we should refrain from actions that resemble adultery and stealing. It's hard to understand how Ibn Ezra could be correct when he suggests that the commandment prohibits particularly pernicious thoughts, outlawing *yetzer hara*.

Instead, the tenth commandment, like the first, can be read not as a commandment at all, but rather a warning: "Beware the evil inclination!" We are enjoined to pay attention to our *yetzer*, to guard against its leading us astray. Those who are most punctilious in observing "You shall not covet" will turn their unhealthy desires to good use—improving their own lives, repairing the world, and serving God.

NOTES

1   Robert Scheer, "Jimmy (Carter), We Hardly Know Y'all," *Playboy*, November 1976.
2   *Babylonian Talmud, Kiddushin* 49b.
3   Scheer, "Jimmy (Carter), We Hardly Know Y'all."
4   Prof. Leonard Greenspoon, "Do Not Covet: Is It a Feeling or an Action?," The Torah.com: A Historical and Contextual Approach, accessed May 13, 2018, https://thetorah.com/do-not-covet-is-it-a-feeling-or-an-action/.
5   Greenspoon, "Do Not Covet."
6   Chizkuni to Exodus 20:14.
7   Nachmanides to Exodus 20:14.
8   *B'reishit Rabbah* 9:7.
9   Rabbi Stephen Fuchs, "A Yom Kippur Carol—Charles Dickens' High Holy Day Sermon," accessed May 13, 2018, scheinerman.net/Judaism/Sermons/fuchs-4.html.
10 Adapted from a story attributed to Jacob ben Wolf Kranz, the Maggid of Dubno (1741–1804).

Conquering and Transforming the Impulse to Want What Is Not Yours

Alan Morinis, PhD

THE TENTH COMMANDMENT STATES, "You shall not covet your neighbor's house: you shall not covet your neighbor's wife, nor male nor female slave, no ox or ass, nor anything that is neighbor's" (Exodus 20:14).

The classic sixteenth-century *mussar* source *Orchot Tzaddikim* underlines the importance of this commandment through a parable about two neighbors whose properties were separated by a wall. One of the men, who coveted his neighbor's wife and possessions, overheard his neighbor saying that he was about to leave on a business trip. What did the covetous man do? He waited until Friday night when everyone was asleep and then broke through the wall between their properties, thus transgressing the commandment "Remember the Sabbath day and keep it holy," since demolition is a prohibited activity on Shabbat. He had sexual relations with his neighbor's wife, violating the commandment "You shall not commit adultery." He then turned to stealing objects from the house (violating "You shall not steal"), at which point the woman was screaming so loudly that he struck and killed her, thereby transgressing "You shall not kill." His parents heard about his misdeeds and confronted him, which led him strike out at them physically, transgressing "Honor your father and your mother." He was eventually brought to court, where he testified that the articles that he took were his all along and he had accidentally killed the woman while retrieving them, violating "You shalt not bear false witness." Wherever he would go, he would swear in God's name that he was innocent, transgressing "You shall not swear falsely by the name of the Eternal your God." Eventually he fell out of society and denounced God altogether, transgressing "I the Eternal am your God." Before long he even took to worshiping idols, transgressing "You shall have no other gods besides Me."

This extended parable is meant to teach a powerful lesson about the importance and danger inherent in coveting. *The tenth commandment is intended to create a bulwark in our inner lives against unethical self-interest, which is not only the source of many forms of transgression, but it is also antithetical to the ultimate value the Torah holds out for us to pursue in our lives: holiness.*

With that much at stake, we would already be well advised to seek ways to avoid transgressing this commandment. But we can draw additional motivation from the fact that one who lusts after another's something is made miserable, rather than happy, by that coveting.

Overcoming covetousness calls for techniques that are different from what would be involved in avoiding forbidden behaviors, however, because this commandment demands that we desist from what is, essentially, an involuntary thought. Abraham ibn Ezra recognized the uniqueness of this aspect of the commandment in the twelfth century, when he commented, "Many people would wonder at this command: How can any person not covet a beautiful thing in one's heart [and] all that appears pleasant in one's eyes?"[1]

The fact is that no one chooses to hanker after that which belongs to another person; at best we recognize the feelings once they have emerged fully formed into consciousness. At worst, it is only after doing something regrettable that we realize what motivated us was lusting after what does not belong to us. In a real sense, coveting is something that happens to us rather than something we choose to do. So how can we escape the grip of coveting?

One surely ineffective option is making a resolution not to covet. That won't work any better than if you were to tell your eyes not to see or your ears not to hear. Coveting is an involuntary response and calls for more sophisticated countermeasures.

Rabbi Yisrael Salanter, who founded the Mussar movement in nineteenth-century Europe, can be our guide here. Like all Mussar teachers, he focused on methodologies for personal inner change and identified three dimensions that can be pursued to inhibit and ultimately transform any inner impulse, such as coveting: *hirgesh*, *kibush*, and *tikkun*.[2]

The first step, called in Hebrew *hirgesh* (literally, "to feel or sense"), involves developing a kind of sensitivity to the inner issue at hand. In the case of coveting, this would involve acknowledging the truth that the thoughts in your mind are actually covetous and recognizing this as a problem.

The step of being sensitive to the issue may seem self-evident and even unnecessary, but it is not so. The coveting impulse can be very powerful and can overwhelm conscience and even rational thought. Rabbi Salanter's call to self-awareness is needed because we human beings are very adept at rationalizing our desires. We can easily convince ourselves that the things we crave are not only permitted to us, but are really due to us, even if they happen to be in someone else's possession at the moment. Wouldn't I take better care of it? Wouldn't I enjoy it more? How happy it would make me!

Rabbi Salanter's necessary first step in contending with coveting involves admitting to yourself with honesty that the feeling exists. Self-reflection and journaling can be effective ways to achieve this *hirgesh*, though the best way is often in conversation with a trusted friend or teacher. Because most of us are masters of self-deception and rationalization, the insights of a friend or teacher can help us bring ourselves to recognition of the truth.

The second stage in the process is called *kibush*, which means "conquering." Once you have succeeded in recognizing the truth about your covetousness, there are concrete actions that can be taken to divert yourself from those thoughts, and hence prevent their enactment. *Kibush* involves training yourself to avoid and to redirect from problematic impulses, as is stated directly by Rabbeinu Bachya[3] in his commentary to the commandment we are exploring:

It is known that coveting something is a matter for the heart. The principal warning contained in this commandment is that one must train oneself to absolutely renounce all hope of ever acquiring things belonging to another person, be it real estate, livestock, inert objects, etc. One must not even think of these and wish for them in one's heart.

The training he suggests is embedded in the final sentence, where he says one must not think of the things one is prone to coveting. As one recent Mussar teacher put it, you are not responsible for seeing the things that cross your field of vision, but you are responsible for the second glance into the rearview mirror.

If you are aware that you desire something that is not yours and that you want to avoid the feelings (and any action they might motivate), the most obvious training of the kind Rabbeinu Bachya mentions you could give yourself would involve sidestepping encounters with whatever it is that triggers that reaction in you. It is an act of will (and hence *kibush*) to walk a route that avoids that person's house or car, or to choose a different class or frequent a different coffee shop where you will not see that person, and so on. Whatever behavior you can change to avoid the stimulus that triggers your coveting falls into this stage of personal self-work.

More subtly, it is possible to train yourself to redirect your unwanted thoughts. The initial step in this process involves preparing an alternative pathway for thoughts that you can open and enter whenever you become aware that unwanted thoughts are beginning to form. This process is a second technique for "conquering" coveting. It again begins with admitting that you are in the grip of coveting, which means that you will know what it is that your thoughts are running after. Then, call an image of that thing to mind, and immediately envision it in a badly deteriorated state. If it is a car, see it in your mind as a total wreck. If it is a building, create an image of it after a fire. Now, equipped with that revised image of the object of coveting, whenever you become aware that thoughts of that kind are coming into your mind, your practice is to choose to call up that alternative image you have prepared, supplanting the problematic one.

These are examples of the *kibush* stage, defined as such because they are acts of will one can undertake to overpower covetous thoughts. At this stage, the impulse to covet is still intact, only it is willfully conquered.

The third and most profoundly transformative step on a Mussar path of changing a trait is named, appropriately enough, *tikkun*, referring to rectifying the impulse itself, so that the feeling of craving does not even arise in the first place.

Above, I quoted Ibn Ezra's question: "Many people would wonder at this command: How can any person not covet a beautiful thing in one's heart?" He actually continues on in that section with something of an answer. He writes, "One should be satisfied with one's lot and not allow one's heart to covet and desire something that is not one's own."[4]

Here we encounter the primary advice of the Mussar teachers for avoiding the trap of coveting altogether. In many cases, where any sort of strong emotion is involved, the Mussar approach does not try to reduce the heat of those emotions, but rather to cultivate other, complementary traits that will have the same effect.

There are two core points that are mentioned frequently in the context of coveting. One is revealed by Ibn Ezra himself when he says that "one should be satisfied with one's lot." This is the inner quality known as *samei'ach b'chelko*, which translates as "happy with one's portion." It is a notion with deep roots, cited twice in *Pirkei Avot*. In 6:6, it is listed as one of the forty-eight methods that facilitate the acquisition of Torah, but in 4:1, we are given some insight into the reward of the trait. Ben Zoma rhetorically asks, "Who is rich?" and answers that the truly wealthy person is "one who is *samei'ach b'chelko* [happy with one's portion]." When we recall the specific things that the Torah counsels us not to covet—our neighbor's wife, slaves, ox, ass, or whatever else belongs to our neighbor—we are counseled to focus our minds and emotions on being happy with our own portion. Celebrating what we have can dissipate the very tendency to covet.

Rather than covet another person's spouse, be happy and celebrate the one you have or might have, or your single status, or whatever happens to be your lot in that area.

Instead of coveting another person's employees, be happy with the ones you have. And that goes for their possessions as well. She drives a Porsche? Be happy with your trusty Ford that ferries you to where you need to go. He wears Armani? Be glad you have decent, functional clothing. Why covet the Rolex when you have your reliable Timex to celebrate?

In place of casting eyes on things that are beyond your reach, see and appreciate whatever it is that you have in your hand right now, because there is surely a gift to be appreciated.

Someone who is prone to coveting is constantly examining what other people have in order to discover who has something superior to what they have. And if that is their inclination, rest assured that there will always be a newer, better, prettier, fancier, more exalted version to crave. But if a person is disposed to rejoice in the gifts already in hand, then coveting isn't even a possibility.

The other approach of this kind involves cultivating the inner trait of *histapkut*, which translates as "sufficiency." The Mussar teachers encourage us to develop an inner sense of what is sufficient on the material plane so that we will have room in our lives to devote ourselves to the higher priority: the spiritual plane. *Histapkut* is all about knowing the difference between what you need and what you want, which is why it has a role in countering covetousness. By definition, coveting does not concern things you justifiably want or need, but rather things you crave illicitly. Living with a commitment to simplicity and sufficiency leaves no room in the mind or heart for the other person's Maserati, spouse, house, or bank account. The eleventh-century Jewish Andalusian poet Shlomo ibn Gavirol reflects on the inner trait of *histapkut*, pointing out that "one who seeks more than one needs hinders himself from enjoying what he has."[5] That is a recipe for a life of unending dissatisfaction and surely, one way or another, the result of coveting.

We can come to coveting when we compare ourselves with other people. What arises in us can lead to resentment, anger, envy, and judgment—attitudes that constrict our hearts and are not godly. When we transform a tendency to covet, we not only protect ourselves from doing illicit and even illegal things, we also release ourselves from the painful grip of unrequited craving. The end result is freedom from harmful thoughts: a step toward bringing more holiness into one's life and into the world.

NOTES

1 Ibn Ezra on Exodus 20:13.
2 Hillel Goldberg, *Israel Salanter: Text, Structure, Idea* (New York: Ktav, 1982), 130–32.
3 Bachya ben Asher ibn Halawa, Spain, 1255–1340.
4 Ibn Ezra, loc. cit.
5 Rabbi Shlomo ibn Gabirol, *Mivchar Peninim*, "*Sha'ar Ha'histapkut*", 155, 161.

Glossary

Adonai. God.

ayin. Nothingness.

baalei HaShem. Masters of the Name.

Baruch HaShem. Blessed is God.

batalah. Nullity, something of little worth, a waste.

Binah. Lit. "Understanding," the third of the ten s'firot.

Birkat Kohanim. The Priestly Blessing found in Numbers 6:24–26.

b'nei aliyah y'chidei s'gulah. Group of learned Jewish mystics.

b'tzelem Elohim. In the image of God.

Chabad. A Jewish Chasidic movement particularly known for outreach.

Chasidism. A spiritual Jewish movement started in Eastern Europe during the eighteenth century based on the teachings of the Baal Shem Tov.

chasidut. Piety.

chayah. Divine Life Force.

Chazal. Acronym for the Hebrew *Chachameinu zichronam livrachah* ("Our Sages, may their memory be blessed"), refers to the classical Jewish Sages.

cherub (pl. cherubim). Angel.

Chesed. Lit. "Loving-kindness," the fourth of the ten s'firot.

chilul HaShem. Profanation of God's name.

Chochmah. Lit. "Wisdom," the second of the ten s'firot.

Daat. Knowledge.

das ganz Andere. Wholly other; used by religion and theology scholar Rudolf Otto (1869–1937) to describe the sacred and ineffable.

das Heilige. The Holy.

Decalogue. Ten Commandments.

ehav et ham'lachah. To love one's occupation.

Ehyeh Asher Ehyeh. God.

Ein Sof. Divine expansiveness, a name of God.

El. God.

Elohim. God.

G'vurah. Lit. "Strength," the fifth of the ten s'firot.

HaKadosh Baruch Hu. "The Holy One, blessed is He," a euphemism for the name of God.

halachah. Rabbinic law.

HaShem. Lit. "The Name," a euphemism for the name of God.

hierophany. Manifestation of the sacred.

histapkut. Contentment, modesty.

hitbod'dut. Self-isolation, self-insulation.

hitbon'nut. Self-examination.

Hod. Lit. "Glory," the eighth of the ten s'firot.

humilitas Dei. Humility of the Divine.

in toto. In total.

jus ad bellum. Just war.

jus in bello. Justice in war.

kabeid. To honor (imperative).

kadosh. Holy, sacred.

kana. Jealous, zealous.

kavod. Glory, honor, respect.

kazav. Something that misleads or disappoints.

Keter. Lit. "Crown," the highest of the ten *s'firot*.

ketubah. Jewish marriage contract.

kibush. Conquering, occupation.

kiddushin. Sanctification of partnership; wedding ceremony.

k'ilu. As though.

kohanim (sing. *kohein*). Priests.

lex talionis. Law of retaliation.

lochem. Warrior.

L'viyim. Levites; biblical tribe of Israel; servants to the *kohanim*.

maaseh. Rabbinic folktale.

machshavah. Thought.

majesta. Majesty.

Malchut. Lit. "Kingdom," the lowest of the ten *s'firot*, also called *Shechinah*.

m'haveh. The aspect of the Divine that renders Pure Being into Being.

midrash. Rabbinic exegesis on biblical text.

mikveh. Traditional Jewish ritual bath.

Minchah. Midday prayer.

mitzvah (pl. *mitzvot*). Commandment, good deed.

m'nuchah. Rest.

mohar. Bridal price.

ner tamid. Eternal flame.

Netzach. Lit. "Eternity," the seventh of the ten *s'firot*.

n'shamah. Soul, spirit.

ratzon. Will.

rodeif. Pursuer.

s'firah (pl. *s'firot*). A divine emanation in Lurianic Kabbalistic theology.

s'firot. System of divine emanations/ attributes of Lurianic Kabbalistic theology.

Shaddai. God.

shav. Vanity, lie.

Shechinah. The (feminine) aspect of God that dwells among the people, another name for *Malchut*.

sheker. Lie, falsehood.

shem. Name.

Shoah. Lit. "Catastrophe," used as the Hebrew name for the Jewish Holocaust of the 1940s.

shomeir. Protector, keeper.

sh'virat hakeilim. Lit. "the breaking of the vessels," a Creation myth of Lurianic Kabbalah in which the light of Creation is too powerful to be contained by clay pots, shattering the vessels.

sine qua non. An essential condition.

takanah. Rabbinic legal ruling.

Tanach. The Jewish canonical Bible, comprising Torah (lit. "Law," the Five Books of Moses), *N'vi-im* (Prophets), and *K'tuvim* (Writings).

Tiferet. Lit. "Adornment," the sixth of the ten *s'firot*.

tikkun. Repair.

tikkun olam. Repairing the world.

tira-u. To respect (imperative).

t'shuvah. Return [to God], repentance.

Tz'vaot. God.

y'chidah. Divine Nonbeing.

yetzer hara. The evil inclination.

YHVH. The Tetragrammaton, the unpronounceable name of God.

Y'sod. Lit. "Foundation," the ninth of the ten *s'firot*.

Yud-Hei-Vav-Hei. The Tetragrammaton, the unpronounceable name of God.

Contributors

Rabbi Oren J. Hayon received his undergraduate education at Rice University and his rabbinical ordination from HUC-JIR in Cincinnati. He has held a number of leadership roles in the Central Conference of American Rabbis, and serves as a frequent editor, translator, and contributor of Hebrew texts and poetry for the CCAR Press. He currently serves on the Editorial Board of *CCAR Journal: The Reform Jewish Quarterly*. Currently, he and his family make their home in Houston, Texas, where he gratefully serves as Senior Rabbi of Congregation Emanu El, and is involved in the leadership of local interfaith, academic, and social service organizations.

Rabbi Richard F. Address, DMin, is founder and director of Jewish Sacred Aging and the website jewishsacredaging.com, and is host of the weekly podcast *Seekers of Meaning.* Ordained by Hebrew Union College–Jewish Institute of Religion in 1972, he served congregations in California and New Jersey as well as over three decades on staff of the Union for Reform Judaism as regional director and as founding director of the Department of Jewish Family Concerns.

Rabbi Annie Belford, a native of El Paso, Texas, received a BA in creative writing from the American Jewish University, an MA in Hebrew letters (MAHL) from Hebrew Union College–Jewish Institute of Religion (New York), and rabbinic ordination in 2004. She has served Temple Sinai since July 2009 as the first woman serving full-time as a solo rabbi in a Houston congregation. She is an avid reader, adores our national parks, and loves nothing more than spending time with her three amazing children.

Rabbi Barry H. Block serves congregation B'nai Israel in Little Rock, Arkansas. A frequent contributor to CCAR Press publications, he is the editor of *The Mussar Torah Commentary* (CCAR Press, 2020). He serves the CCAR on its Board of Trustees.

Rabbi Darcie Crystal teaches leadership and runs the Summer Residency Program for rabbinical students at Hebrew Union College–Jewish Institute of Religion (HUC-JIR). She teaches Exploring Judaism at Central Synagogue in New York City. She has served congregations including Temple Beth-El of Great Neck and Tamid: The Downtown Synagogue. She is a Rabbis Without Borders Fellow and sits on the Board of Directors of Moving Traditions and on the CCAR Ethics Committee. She received her BA from Princeton University and her MAHL and ordination from HUC-JIR.

Rabbi Geoffrey W. Dennis serves Congregation Kol Ami, in Flower Mound, Texas, where he styles himself the "Chief Rabbi of Denton County." He also teaches Bible and Kabbalah in the Jewish and Israel Studies Program at the University of North Texas. He is the author of two books, *The Encyclopedia of Jewish Myth, Magic, and Mysticism* (2nd edition, 2015) and *Sefer Ha-Bahir: The Book of Brilliance* (2017), as well as numerous articles, encyclopedia entries, and book chapters. He and his wife Robin have two twenty-something sons they are easing out of the house.

Rabbi Joshua Feigelson, PhD, is Executive Director of the Institute for Jewish Spirituality. He has previously served as Dean of Students in the Divinity School at the University of Chicago. He was the founder and executive director of Ask Big Questions, an initiative developed by Hillel International that was awarded the inaugural Lippman-Kanfer Prize for Applied Jewish Wisdom. He earned his PhD in religious studies from Northwestern University, where he served as the Hillel rabbi from 2005 to 2011. He holds rabbinic ordination from YCT Rabbinical School.

Rabbi Mordecai Finley, PhD, is the spiritual leader of Ohr Ha-Torah Synagogue, a traditional-progressive synagogue, in Mar Vista, California. He is also a professor of Jewish thought at the Academy for Jewish Religion, California campus, where he has taught Jewish mysticism, spiritual psychology, and Jewish liturgy, among other topics. He also has a counseling practice and offers seminars on the wisdom and virtue dimensions of spiritual psychology.

Rabbi Reuven Firestone, PhD, is the Regenstein Professor in Medieval Judaism and Islam at Hebrew Union College–Jewish Institute of Religion and affiliate professor at the USC School of Religion. Author of eight books and over one hundred scholarly articles on Judaism, Islam, and their relationship with one another and Christianity, he lectures in the United States, Europe, Asia, and the Middle East. He is active on the boards of numerous scholarly journals and boards and commissions engaged in interreligious relations and dialogue. He served as vice president of the Association for Jewish Studies and as president of the International Qur'anic Studies Association.

Rabbi Eliana Fischel was ordained in 2018 by Hebrew Union College-Jewish Institute of Religion. She is currently an assistant rabbi at Washington Hebrew Congregation where she focuses on engaging teens, 20/30s, and young couples. While at HUC-JIR, she was a Bonnie and Daniel Tisch Rabbinic Fellow, as well as a Roswell Klal Yisrael Fellow. She wrote her rabbinic thesis on polyamory and Judaism, entitled, "How Open Is Our Tent? Polyamorous Relationships in the Jewish Context."

Rabbi Laura Geller, ordained in 1976, is rabbi emerita of Temple Emanuel of Beverly Hills. She was twice named one of *Newsweek*'s "50 Most Influential Rabbis in America." A founder of the first synagogue-based village, ChaiVillageLA, she was named by Next Avenue as one of the "50 Influencers in Aging" in 2017. She is the author with her late husband, Richard Siegel, of *Getting Good at Getting Older* (2019).

Rabbi Kari Hofmaister Tuling, PhD, received her rabbinic ordination in 2004 and earned her PhD in Jewish thought in 2013, both from Hebrew Union College–Jewish Institute of Religion in Cincinnati. She currently serves Congregation Kol Haverim in Glastonbury, a suburb of Hartford, Connecticut. She is the author of *Thinking about God: Jewish Views*, a book on Jewish theology.

Rabbi Rachel Kahn-Troster is deputy director of T'ruah: The Rabbinic Call for Human Rights. Ordained in 2008 by the Jewish Theological Seminary, she is a nationally recognized leader and expert on human rights issues such as fighting forced labor and ending mass incarceration and solitary confinement. At T'ruah, she leads the #TomatoRabbis campaign, bringing Jewish communal support to the Fair Food Program of the Coalition of Immokalee Workers, and was a founder of the Worker-Driven Social Responsibility Network.

Rabbi Michael Marmur, PhD, was ordained in the Israeli Rabbinic Program of Hebrew Union College–Jewish Institute of Religion (HUC-JIR). He is associate professor of Jewish theology at HUC-JIR Jerusalem, having served previously as the dean of the campus there and subsequently as provost of HUC-JIR.

Alan Morinis, PhD, is the founder of The Mussar Institute and an active interpreter of the teachings and practices of the Mussar tradition, about which he regularly gives lectures and workshops. Born and raised in a culturally Jewish but non-observant home, he studied social anthropology at Oxford University on a Rhodes Scholarship, earning his doctorate at that university. He has written books and produced films and documentaries and has taught at several universities. For the past nineteen years the nearly lost Jewish spiritual discipline of Mussar has been his passion, a journey recorded in the book *Climbing Jacob's Ladder* (2002). His guide to Mussar, entitled *Everyday Holiness: The Jewish Spiritual Path of Mussar*, was published in 2007 and became a best-selling handbook to Mussar for this generation. His guide to Mussar practice, *Every Day, Holy Day*, came out in 2010. His newest book, *With Heart in Mind*, was published in 2014.

Rabbi Harold L. Robinson, DDiv, DHL, Rear Admiral CHC U.S. Navy Ret, was ordained in 1974 by Hebrew Union College–Jewish Institute of Religion, Cincinnati, accepted a reserve commission in the Navy Chaplain Corps, and assigned to marine units. He has served congregations Temple Israel, Gary, Indiana (1974–77); Cape Cod Synagogue, Hyannis, Massachusetts (1977–98); and B'nai Zion, Shreveport, Louisiana (1998–2005); and as deputy chief of chaplains in the United States Navy (2004–7) and Marine Corps (2004–7). Following 9/11, he deployed on several occasions with US Naval Forces in the Persian Gulf, and with US Marines in Iraq and Afghanistan. He was awarded the Distinguished Service Medal.

Roberta Rosenthal Kwall, JD, is the Raymond P. Niro Professor at DePaul University College of Law. She is an internationally renowned scholar and lecturer on topics relating to Jewish law and culture, authorship rights, and intellectual property. Her books include *Remix Judaism: Preserving Tradition in a Diverse World* (2020), *The Myth of the Cultural Jew* (2015), and *The Soul of Creativity* (2010). She also teaches a course about Judaism in America at Radzyner Law School in Israel.

Kenneth Seeskin, PhD, is professor of philosophy and Philip M. and Ethel Klutznick Professor of Jewish Civilization at Northwestern University. Over his more than forty years as an academic, he has served as chair of the Philosophy Department and the Religious Studies Department. He has published numerous books and articles on Maimonides. His most recent book, *Thinking about the Torah: A Philosopher Reads the Bible*, will be followed by *Thinking about the Prophets*.

Tiffany Shlain, honored by *Newsweek* as one of the "Women Shaping the 21st Century," is an Emmy-nominated filmmaker, author, and founder of the Webby Awards. Selected by the Albert Einstein Foundation for *Genius: 100 Visions of the Future*, Tiffany's films and work have received over eighty awards and distinctions, including premieres at the Sundance Film Festival. She is the author of *24/6: The Power of Unplugging One Day a Week* (2019).

Rabbi Jonathan Siger currently serves Congregation Jewish Community North in Spring, Texas. A graduate of Brandeis University, Hebrew Union College–Jewish Institute of Religion, and the Second City Conservatory of Improvisational Theater, Rabbi Siger is also a certified law enforcement chaplain specializing in patrol and critical stress incidents. He has written several pieces for *Men's Health* without a trace of irony. In addition to his rabbinical and chaplaincy obligations, Siger is an associate of Hillel at Texas A&M University. He lives in suburban Houston with his wife Jennifer and their two children, Azriel and Gavriella, and their dog, Daisy May.

Elsie R. Stern, PhD, is the Vice President for Academic Affairs and Associate Professor of Bible at the Reconstructionist Rabbinical College. She is the author of *From Rebuke to Consolation: Exegesis and Theology in the Liturgical Anthology of the Ninth of Av*, co-editor of *The Dictionary of the Bible in Ancient Media*, and is a contributor to the *Jewish Study Bible* and *Women's Torah Commentary*. Her teaching and research focus on the performance, transmission, and reception of Torah within ancient and contemporary Jewish communities.

Batya Ungar-Sargon, PhD, is the op-ed editor of the *Forward*. Her work has appeared in the *New York Times*, the *Washington Post*, and *Foreign Policy*.

Rabbi Dr. Shmuly Yanklowitz is the president and dean of the Valley Beit Midrash (Jewish pluralistic adult learning and leadership), the founder and president of Uri L'Tzedek (Jewish social justice), the founder and CEO of SHAMAYIM (Jewish animal advocacy), the founder and president of YATOM (Jewish foster and adoption network), and the author of seventeen books on Jewish ethics. *Newsweek* named him one of the top fifty rabbis in America, and the *Forward* named him one of the fifty most influential American Jews. Rabbi Shmuly, his wife, four children, and foster children live in Scottsdale, Arizona.